Vivian is a woman who definitely splashes God's love all over. Her heart is so tender toward the lost, broken, and disenfranchised. In this book you will not only be inspired, but also motivated and empowered to reach out and let your love splash all over too!

Dr. Patricia King
patriciakingmentor.com

Splashing is such a good word to describe God's heart to demonstrate His love, especially to those who have been overlooked or forgotten. It is the picture of extreme overflow of the supernatural goodness of the Father to a hurting and lost generation. He wants the masses to know that each and every person is so valuable to Him … so much so that He would pay the highest price of heaven to reveal His passion, His only Son! I have had the great joy of partnering with Vivian and her vision to love people to Jesus. I highly recommend this book that not only comes from her heart, but also comes from her practical experiences of sharing who Jesus is to the streets of our city!

Pastor Mike Smith
Redeeming Love Church, Maplewood, MN

Splash All Over masterfully combines sound, biblical insight with powerful God stories from Vivian's radical lifestyle of love. The valuable wisdom and impartation within this book make it a must read for this generation!

Katharine G. Racine
All People's Church

Vivian Klebs shows us how an open and willing heart can change lives. Her stories and examples are so inspirational, and they create in the reader a longing to be more intentional in sharing the love of God. Vivian's passion for the lost comes from a place of love and compassion, and she teaches how this is the most important motivator a person can have. Whether you're comfortable with sharing the love of God with others, or if you wish you were more intentional, this book is for you.

Rev. Denise Siemens
Founder at Arise! Women and ElevateHER®

Vivian found us in the prayer room at our campus college shop while on a treasure hunt ten years ago. She is consistently the best we've ever worked with in sharing the Good News in practical, prophetic ways. God has gifted her to flow with the Holy Spirit in equipping even the very new and uncomfortable believers to step out and join the fun. That experience is the basis of this wonderful book. Vivian's very presence brings out the gold in all those who surround her. She uses a simple approach that takes away the fear that many have toward evangelism. This book will propel you forward all the while calling out your identity, teaching you how to listen to Holy Spirit for direction, and how to use every tool available to you. Vivian's passion for reaching the lost is contagious. So get splashing!

John & Jen Tolo
GodTown, Twin Cities, MN

SPLASH
ALL OVER

TAKING GOD'S POWER AND LOVE TO THE STREETS

VIVIAN STRONG KLEBS

Splash All Over
Copyright © 2017 Vivian Strong Klebs

ISBN-13: 978-1981312405

Cover by Yvonne Parks at pearcreative.ca
Interior by Ryan Adair at missiowriting.com

Printed in the United States of America

This book is dedicated to my wonderful and loving husband, and to my children and friends who have cheered me on. It is also dedicated to my future grandchildren who will be world changers and history makers, splashing love everywhere they go.

Contents

SECTION 2: TOOLS

Introduction

The Church has taken many approaches to evangelism. Regardless of our approach, we must learn how to give away God's love in a tangible and effective manner with compassion, as Jesus did. Jesus' Kingdom is about new life and transformation.

Recently, I was at a park with some friends sharing God's love with people. My friends and I were on an adventure with the Holy Spirit, who was our guide to finding "divine appointments."

We noticed three teens sitting on a park bench together, looking very bored. As we approached them, I could sense, more than boredom, an atmosphere of depression and hopelessness. Usually it's awkward to approach strangers and just start talking. However, I find that as the Spirit leads, it is possible to engage people in conversation out of love and obedience without expectations.

The teens were hesitant at first, but they warmed up when we told them that we were on a treasure hunt with God—and that *they* were God's treasures. This piqued their interest! No one had ever told them before they were God's treasures. As we engaged them in conversation, we listened to their hearts. The two young men were more open with us than the young woman was; she was visibly distant and angry. She had a tough wall of protection around her heart and her demeanor portrayed this.

I asked the boys if I could pray a blessing over them. As I prayed over the boys, I sensed God's heart of love, and He gave me some simple, prophetic words for one of them. I told him, "God wants to be your Daddy."

He replied, "I never knew my dad. He left my mom and me when I was two." I explained that God wanted to heal his wounded heart and be a good Papa to him—to provide for him and protect him and call out his true identity—to have a loving relationship with him. We could sense the Holy Spirit's peace, and so could he. Soon he experienced God's presence melting his hard heart and he asked Jesus into his life. He had tears in his eyes and a big smile on his face as that inner joy of the Holy Spirit gave him new hope.

The other young man smiled at his friend's transformation and then he started to share his heart with us. He, too, had never known his dad and he had longed for a father figure. He told us he had just gotten out of jail and that he had asked Jesus into his life while in jail. Jesus had replaced his loneliness, unforgiveness, and hurt with new trust for God and people. Even so, his big smile was hiding depression, anger, and rejection. He asked if we would pray for him, as he needed a job and hope for his future. We prayed a blessing over him, and we added prophetic words of hope, comfort, and encouragement. When we finished, he said he felt renewed hope that the God of the universe had given him a purpose and new destiny. God had affirmed the words of Jeremiah 29:11 in his heart: "'For I know the plans I have for you,' says the Lord. 'They are plans for good and not for disaster, to give you a future and a hope'" (Jeremiah 29:11, NLT).

The girl who was with them appeared to be angry and said she was not interested in having us pray over her. However, when the two boys told her how amazing the peace that they felt was and that she should, "try it, you'll like it," we could feel God's tangible presence in their concern and compassion for her. Reluctantly, she agreed that we could pray. As we began to pray, the Spirit revealed to me that she had a wounded and grieving heart because she had lost someone very dear to her and had put a wall around her heart to protect herself. My heart ached for her. The Holy Spirit opened her heart. She explained that she had been excited to be pregnant, but her baby had recently died at birth. She was mad at God and blamed Him for her baby's death. I asked her if she would like to feel God's peace and she said yes. The other two offered to pray out loud with her so she wouldn't be embarrassed to speak out. All three of them prayed together out loud and God's loving presence became very strong.

He had definitely directed us to these three broken hearts so that His Holy Spirit could heal them. Jesus said:

> The Spirit of the Lord is upon Me, because He has anointed Me to preach the gospel to the poor; He has sent Me to heal the brokenhearted, to proclaim liberty to the captives and recovery of sight to the blind, to set at liberty those who are oppressed. (Luke 4:18)

He came over two thousand years ago and He comes today to restore the relationship of the Father to His beloved sons and daughters.

* * * * *

I have two friends who go to bus transit stations, and as people get on and off the bus, they approach them and ask them to read Romans 10:9–10 (NIV): "If you declare with your mouth, 'Jesus is Lord,' and believe in your heart that God raised him from the dead, you will be saved. For it is with your heart that you believe." Then they ask, "Have you ever confessed Jesus as Lord of your life?" It is amazing how many people respond positively as they lead them in a prayer to repent of their sins and ask Jesus to be in charge of their lives. They have seen many people pray this prayer and as they watch, the Holy Spirit moves in them. When they approach people in love, people can feel and sense that this love is real. People are so hungry for hope and peace, and Jesus brings both.

Whether we approach strangers for salvation or with wonderful miracles, as long as we are doing it in love, God will bring people to Himself and show them His plan for their lives. People are so hungry for meaning in their lives, right here and now; they are usually just one miracle away from complete transformation.

Transformation may consist of a saving change of heart, being set free from addictions, or whatever personal miracle God has in mind. People may be healed or delivered from evil spirits. They may be strengthened by hearing words of affirmation and hope and discovering the faith to believe that they are true. This is not just a "feel good" Gospel. In a real sense, this is moving people from one kingdom to another, to God's Kingdom of love and power.

*   *   *   *

My oldest daughter worked for a large international software company that hired immigrants to valet-park the office workers' cars off campus. Soon, she got to know on a first-name basis many of the valet attendants from different nations. She has always had a "heart for the nations," so it was natural for her to take an interest in them. She would ask them about their families and remember their names. Sometimes she would take them cookies. One day they saw her coming and skipped everyone in line ahead of her to get to her car, and then excitedly greeted her. Her boss was ahead of her in line and was shocked by this special treatment. Later he joked, "Who do you think you are?"

When she told me about it, Isaiah 55:5 came to my mind: "Surely you shall call a nation you do not know, and nations who do not know you shall run to you, because of the Lord your God, and the Holy One of Israel; for He has glorified you."

Surely the nations will come running as we show God's love and kindness to them!

*   *   *   *

What is the common element in each of these stories?

It is God's great love and compassion for people (which He displayed when Jesus died on the cross) revealed through the willing hearts of believers who carry His love and give it away.

Any method of evangelism is great if you do it in the power of the Holy Spirit and people feel loved. You can use Bible verses, prophetic words, testimonies, healing or other supernatural signs. When people sense God's presence and His compassion for them, their hearts become open to Him.

It is the Holy Spirit's job, not ours, to bring conviction to people's hearts. He is able to bring the weight of sin crashing down on someone as they see a loving God who has provided a way out of this cycle of shame and hopelessness. He offers the Light of Jesus shining through in supernatural ways to bring conviction and repentance.

The Holy Spirit wants to use each of us to powerfully affect our sphere of influence. But each of us must live a *lifestyle* of love, not just reach out to others at an evangelistic event. To do that, we need to find out how to be equipped, how to be full to overflowing with God's great love. You can't give away what you don't have.

Every heart *can* be ready to encounter Jesus' love. However, because of life experiences, not every heart *is* ready. Religiously trying to lead people to a relationship with Jesus doesn't work, and it can be abrasive or non-productive, at best. No one has ever been argued into the Kingdom. Each of us has a small part to play, and the only way we can do it is to listen to and obey the Holy Spirit. Sometimes He leads us to pick ripe fruit and other times He helps us sow seeds for a future harvest.

6

Introduction

And the harvest is at hand. We are living in a harvest season, and people are hungry for the supernatural—either heavenly or occult. Any list of best-selling books reveals this preoccupation with supernatural things. For our part, we need to know how to discern God's presence and how to do only what we see the Father doing—just as Jesus did.

How, then, do we do this? How do we get equipped for this great adventure? What are some ways to give this love away? How do we become aware of "divine appointments"?

In the following chapters, I will lead you through what I have found to be the most effective ways to touch others with the love of God and reach them for Christ. God wants to fill you with His love so that fear does not hold you back from helping others to know the extravagant love of God. It's time to splash His love all over.

"For God has not given us a spirit of fear, but of power and of love and of a sound mind" (2 Timothy 1:7).

Application Prayer

Start out by praying this simple prayer out loud, as there is power in hearing your own voice declare and decree these words:

Father, I want to have a teachable and obedient heart. Open the eyes of my heart to see all that you have in store for me on this great adventure. Please give me divine appointments and highlight in the Spirit all with whom you want me to engage. Give me sure-footed confidence in you alone to step out in love, faith and power. In Jesus' name, amen.

7

Section 1

Established in Love

Chapter 1

Extravagant God

"God so loved the world that He gave. . . ." We have been created in His image to give away (splash) His amazing love over everyone we encounter.

One of the best-known Bible verses ever is John 3:16, which says, "God so loved the world that He gave His only begotten Son, that whoever believes in Him should not perish but have everlasting life." Love is the beginning, middle, and end of all that God does. Only an extravagant God would give His only Son to die for people like us.

We have been created in His image. Therefore, filled with His love, we will naturally splash love all over everyone we encounter. Our lifestyle becomes one of introducing people to Jesus. We can expect boundless possibilities from our extravagantly loving, kind, good, and faithful God.

This sounds so simple. Why then do the vast majority of believers have so much difficulty taking His love outside the church walls?

Love That Creates, Comforts and Covers

In the beginning, God created the world and all that's in it. He loved His creation and knew each one of us before we ever appeared on earth. He has always wanted to have an intimate relationship with each of us.

God is so full of love that He can't help but give. Unfortunately, people in our culture often view God as a legalistic Father who only wants to correct their behavior. How can we show them the real God, a gracious, kind and loving Daddy who created us to be loved by Him?

My mother was raised on a farm in the foothills of northeastern Alabama. Her father died of typhoid fever when she was just ten years old. This left her mother to raise six young children alone. My mother would tell the story of going to school one cold day when there was a light snow, which was unusual for Alabama. She and her siblings didn't have many warm clothes, so they were told to not walk home at lunch time as was their custom. As lunchtime approached, here came her mother and grandfather with a bucket of hot sweet potatoes wrapped in a quilt to keep them warm. Everyone in the little schoolhouse had hot sweet potatoes and butter that day for lunch. My mother knew that how much love and dedication this showed; her arthritic grandfather had to hitch up the wagon and her mother had to bake all those potatoes from her meager food supply in order to bring them to the children.

To this day in our family when we taste sweet potatoes, we taste love, because of my mother's fond memory. Was I there when this happened, cold and hungry? No, of course not. But my mother had very few precious memories of this time in her life, and this was one she cherished. Every time she would share this story, I could feel the love. I would be covered in love as the quilt covered the sweet potatoes to keep them warm.

This is what God's great love for us does. He gave His beloved Son, whom all of heaven adores, to die for us even before we were born so that we could choose life. Now that's unconditional love!

Since God is love, everything He creates is created in love and everything He does is full of love.

* * * * *

A young woman named Amy asked if we could go out together on a treasure hunt like the one I described in the Introduction. Before a treasure hunt, you ask the Holy Spirit to give you clues, and then you follow the clues to look for people with whom you can share God's love. We decided to meet in the evening at the large Mall of America in Bloomington, Minnesota, near where we live.

Amy started to get cold feet. She told me later that she felt really scared and awkward and didn't know what she was supposed to do or say. She had worked all day, had a headache, and almost cancelled. But out of courtesy to me, knowing I had already driven to the mall, she came anyway.

We prayed on a bench inside the mall and asked the Holy Spirit for clues so that we could hunt for God's treasures (people). Amy, nervous about approaching strangers, rolled her eyes and said, "I don't hear a thing." Despite her lack of clues, I felt I had gotten a clue about where to go—"food court." We headed that way.

Once we got to the food court, we looked around and spotted a young couple deep in conversation. The girl was thin, with several tattoos and piercings and a very creative hairstyle. He was African-American and was wearing several silver bracelets. The two of them appeared to be engrossed in a very serious conversation.

I pointed out this couple and asked Amy if she wanted to approach them. She spotted the couple, her eyes got big and she said, "This is way outside my comfort zone. OK . . . Let's go for it."

We went over to the couple, commented on their creativity and style, and engaged them in conversation. As they warmed up to us, we asked if they would like prayer for anything or if we could pray a blessing over them. They were reluctant at first, because they said they had been hurt by the church and religious people, but they gave their consent. As we prayed a blessing, I sensed that the woman was a dancer. Thinking of a line from a worship song, I told her that she had been made to "dance over injustice." I asked her if she liked to dance and she glanced over at her boyfriend and hesitantly said, "yes."

After giving them a few encouraging words, we parted ways. As we were walking away, Amy stopped and blurted out, "She's pregnant and dances in a strip club. I have to go back and talk to her." This was an unexpected prophetic word of knowledge.

We turned around. By now, the couple was no longer sitting in the food court. We spotted the young lady walking away with a girlfriend way down the mall. Amy took off running, with me in hot pursuit, thinking, "I sure hope she's right with this or it could be embarrassing."

By the time we caught up with the young lady, Amy was crying because she was so overcome with the presence of the Holy Spirit. She had been hesitant and uncertain before, but now she had been overtaken by God's love and had to give it away. She got the girl's attention, explaining, "This may sound awkward, but I have a question to ask."

The girl could see that Amy was very emotional and kindly said, "Sure."

Amy asked, "Are you pregnant?" The girl looked down at her flat stomach and said, "Do I look pregnant?" But then she started crying, too, saying, "Yes, I just found out that I am pregnant." She was scared and didn't know what to do now. Amy then said, "and you dance in a club, right?" Now they were both crying.

The girl said that she and her boyfriend had been discussing what to do when we approached them in the food court. She said, "Have you ever seen a pregnant pole dancer? No. Now I will get fired or have to quit." She told us that she had no means of supporting herself, her boyfriend was unemployed, and she was scared.

This word of knowledge opened the door for Amy to share further with this young woman how God loves her and the baby and knows everything about her. She prayed right in the mall, in front of her girlfriend, asking Jesus to come into her heart and inviting the Holy Spirit be in control. We encouraged her to seek out some support from a local Christian Pregnancy Crisis

Center. Her heart changed from fear to love in a matter of moments as she was comforted with His love.

She became Facebook friends with Amy and later explained that she and her boyfriend had been contemplating aborting the baby. After Amy shared her word of knowledge about the pregnancy, she reasoned that if God knew about this baby, then she would be OK giving birth. She even invited Amy to her baby shower.

A new life was spared and covered in a blanket of love by a great Creator God who hears our every sigh:

> Praise be to the God and Father of our Lord Jesus
> Christ, the Father of compassion and the God of all
> comfort, who comforts us in all our troubles, so that
> we can comfort those in any trouble with the comfort
> we ourselves receive from God. For just as we share
> abundantly in the sufferings of Christ, so also our
> comfort abounds through Christ.
> (2 Corinthians 1:3–5, NIV)

Unconditional Love or Performance-Based Love?

God's unconditional love covers us in the midst of real-life issues. His kindness leads to repentance, not to condemnation or judgment. When you picture God, do you see an angry, finger-pointing, demanding God or a loving Father who desires to create a safe, loving place and comfort you in the midst of all hurts, covering you under His protective arms?

> Don't you see how wonderfully kind, tolerant, and
> patient God is with you? Does this mean nothing to

you? Can't you see that his kindness is intended to turn you from your sin? (Romans 2:4, NLT)

He will cover you with his feathers, and under his wings you will find refuge; his faithfulness will be your shield and rampart. You will not fear the terror of night, nor the arrow that flies by day, nor the pestilence that stalks in the darkness, nor the plague that destroys at midday. (Psalm 91:3–6, NIV)

People are tired of performance-based love. They are thirsty for unconditional love that brings peace, love, and joy. Performance-based love is never enough. It demands more and more. In the end, it is insatiable; it can't ever be satisfied. Performance-based love makes us give up. It leaves us feeling as if we will never be able to meet its demands . . . so why bother? The enemy of our souls has planted this false idea of God, replacing a loving Papa with a distant and unapproachable Judge who demands ever-stricter observance of His impossible expectations.

Extravagant God Versus God of Law

The basic theme is the same in both the Old and New Testament: Today, choose life or death. How do we know what to do and how to do it? Because God has given us the answer: "Choose life" (Deuteronomy 30:19). Jesus is Life. He couldn't have made it clearer when He said, "I am the way, the truth, and the life. No one comes to the Father except through Me" (John 14:6).

In the Old Testament, God, set up a standard (the Law) for obedience. In Deuteronomy 28, He says that obedience brings blessings and disobedience brings curses. This is a definite choice between life and death. In the New Testament, Jesus fulfilled the Law and brought blessings to all who would come under His banner of love, so that our Father now views us through the lens of Jesus-colored glasses. The realization of how much we are loved, despite our mistakes and failures, enkindles in us a new desire to give this unconditional love away to others. The news about Jesus is called Good News because it's the best news this planet has ever known.

This Good News about unconditional love results in extravagance on God's part. That is why we can expect such amazing outpourings from Him. That is why He invites us to dream big with Him and join in believing, "with God all things are possible" (Matthew 19:26).

Love Is Tangible

When my children were preschoolers, we read a book together called *Jesse Bear, What Will You Wear?* This story taught little ones to dress appropriately for the season and weather. Children tend to dress according to how they feel. They love to wear new rain boots and a favorite shirt no matter what the weather. As adults, we wake up in the morning and look out the window or check our phones to see what the weather will be like for the day. We dress for the weather to stay dry, warm, or cool.

Wearing *love* is always in season and fashionable. It is always the right season for wearing tangible love. As a prophetic act, choose to put on love, and it will get you through all kinds of stormy weather. It is always in style.

> Therefore, as God's chosen people, holy and dearly loved, clothe yourselves with compassion, kindness, humility, gentleness and patience. (Colossians 3:12, NIV)

> Christ [will] dwell in your hearts through faith. And I pray that you, being rooted and established in love, may have power, together with all the Lord's holy people, to grasp how wide and long and high and deep is the love of Christ, and to know this love that surpasses knowledge—that you may be filled to the measure of all the fullness of God. (Ephesians 3:17–19, NIV)

Never the Same after Encountering the Love of God

We are never the same after encountering God's love through Jesus. From then on, we can change the atmosphere just by declaring God's love and exploits, and we can draw people into a new dimension. Like attracts like; negative speech attracts misfortune and positive speech attracts love. Sometimes you can actually feel the atmosphere change to one of love and acceptance when you unleash your heart of love.

Peter's shadow healed people because it held something tangible (see Acts 5:15). We carry a presence of love and hope that people can actually feel and discern. They also can discern any negative or judgmental attitudes. His love will naturally attract the people who are weary and thirsty for something so tangible.

Compassion versus Religious Spirit

Many times in the New Testament, we read that Jesus had compassion. His compassion led him to feed the hungry, heal the sick, raise the dead, or do whatever was needed. For example, "Jesus saw the huge crowd as he stepped from the boat, and he had compassion on them because they were like sheep without a shepherd. So he began teaching them many things" (Mark 6:34, NLT).

We have compassion on pre-believers because we want them to know the truth, and this compassion drives us to expend our energy on their behalf. One time, I was in Belize on a mission trip with some students. We were at a sweet little country church and all of us were speaking out words of knowledge from the front. I could see a fragile-looking woman with a toddler asleep in her arms. As word after word was called out, she tried to raise her hand but the child was asleep on her good arm. I noticed that something was wrong with her right arm and she couldn't lift it. I could see the look of desperation on her face as she thought she was getting passed by. Someone spoke out a word of knowledge that God wanted to heal an arm and shoulder so I walked over to pray for her. As I sat down beside her, I noticed that she had cigar or cigarette burns on her arm, and bruises. I sensed a spirit of abuse. We didn't speak the same language but as I prayed, I sensed that the pain she carried was deeper than her hurting arm. As I asked the Lord to please heal her arm, I felt His compassion and great love for this little brokenhearted mother. I put my arms around her and felt this intense fiery love going between us. No words were needed as we cried together over His great love. I sensed that the Lord was saying, "Some wounds are deeper than just skin deep but my love heals all." She received both inner healing and physical healing without any words having passed between us. We didn't speak the same human language but we did speak the language of God's great healing love.

A religious spirit will stir up criticism or judgment regarding what God is doing. It happened to Jesus:

> Tax collectors and other notorious sinners often came to listen to Jesus teach. This made the Pharisees and teachers of religious law complain that he was associating with such sinful people—even eating with them! (Luke 14:1–2, NLT)

Some things haven't changed much. The religious spirit is subtle and invites us to take offense, if not on our own behalf, then on behalf of others or even God Himself. But compassion invites us to put on love and to behave accordingly.

* * * * *

I was at an outreach in New Orleans during Mardi Gras with 300 college-age young adults. We were out on Jackson Square getting ready to have a drum corps perform and do some line dancing to attract a crowd. We had music, a DJ who gave his testimony, and people stationed in the crowd to share with others. We also had signs that said, "Free Spiritual Readings."

When we arrived to set up, I noticed a religious couple with a bullhorn and a sign that said, "God hates fornicators, adulterers, homosexuals, and revelers." They were angry. The more they yelled, the more they attracted a group of other haters, people carrying really nasty signs that would offend most people. As the haters tried to out-yell each other, the drum corps began and drowned them out.

Soon, a large crowd gathered and began clapping and participating. After everyone did some fun line dances, the DJ gave a powerful testimony about how he came from brokenness to life because of Jesus' love. He offered this love to everyone in the crowd and asked those of us with the group to raise our hands so people could approach us with questions about this love. We had many people to pray with to receive God's great forgiveness and to be reconciled with Him and join the family of God.

One man asked, "Does God really hate me? I am gay."

He was told, "Of course not, He died for you and me while we were yet in sin. He might not always like what we do but He always loves us and will forgive us." And, "Only God's love through Jesus and the Holy Spirit power can give you the desire and the power to change your lifestyle."

I walked over to try to tell the religious couple that we were a group of believers also—part of the family. The man was not even approachable, his anger was so palpable, so I went over to the woman instead. As I said a few words, she hissed at me,

"You people are evil." My immediate reaction was to want to call out that religious spirit and to curse her right back. However, I realized that the religious spirit was tempting me to be just as critical and judgmental as she was. So I turned and walked away, forgiving and blessing her. Only the Holy Spirit will be able to convince her that God loves her beyond her wildest imagination. Only He can transform the human heart. Only He can replace our hatred, criticism, and judgment with so much transforming love that we want to give it away.

Love Covers a Multitude of Sins

King David said, "I have looked for You in the sanctuary, to see Your power and Your glory. Because Your lovingkindness is better than life, my lips shall praise You" (Psalm 63:2–3).

We put our hope in His unfailing love. His covenant of love is unbreakable. He is known as the His-love-endures-forever God. It is no coincidence that the great love chapter, 1 Corinthians 13, comes before the chapter that tells us to seek after spiritual gifts: "Follow the way of love and eagerly desire gifts of the Spirit, especially prophecy" (1 Corinthians 14:1, NIV).

If we can't go in love, we need not go at all. We can't give away what we don't have. When we get out on the streets, we need to know that all of heaven is backing us because of His great love. Lovers always get more accomplished than servants. Lovers move and operate in love. As we dispense love everywhere, it naturally transforms us from being people who are striving and performance-based to people who are champions—of love.

Application Prayer

Lord, thank you for loving me and giving me life in your Son, Jesus. I want to be filled to overflowing with your love. Let my heart burn with compassion for people as Jesus' heart did and does. Break my heart for what breaks yours. Holy Spirit, come and be like a river of love flowing from my innermost being. In Jesus' name, amen.

Chapter 2

Identity as Champions

Identity comes from knowing who we are as beloved sons and daughters, not from our performance or striving. You can't give away what you don't have.

One time, I asked the Lord for revelation concerning street evangelism, when you have people pray a salvation prayer but you know you will never see them again and certainly will not be able to disciple them. I heard, "Are you the author and finisher of their faith?" No, of course not. I knew that God was telling me to trust that the One who has begun a good work will take care of finishing it. I felt that the Holy Spirit was expressing the sentiment: "I will take care of this." This was a great relief to me as a "recovering religious person" who thought it was my job to fix people. He also reminded me that this is about love and heart knowledge more than head knowledge. What a relief to let the Holy Spirit do what He does best, to work in people's lives to bring them into a heart knowledge of Jesus Christ and a relationship with a loving Father. He would bring them into the great adventure of being discipled into His Kingdom.

I had the honor and privilege of speaking at a church in Brazil after a women's conference. Several women had brought their husbands to church for the first time that Sunday. When I was ministering afterward, a man in a police uniform came and fell at my feet, sobbing. The interpreter told me he was known for having many girlfriends and cheating on his wife, as was acceptable in his macho culture. He confessed and repented of his sins and the Lord told me to tell him, "You are not your past. Go forward as a mighty man of God focusing on loving your family as Jesus loves you."

I didn't have to tell him to feel guilty or make him repent over and over. The Holy Spirit brings conviction and propels people into a new ability to move forward in love. I *did* need to be sure of my own identity as a beloved daughter of God because knowing our own identity allows us to call out the gold in others and not the dirt. When I know that God has forgiven me, I can offer His forgiveness to others.

Religion will never compel anyone to straighten up and fly right, but a relationship with a loving Jesus brings both the motivation and the power to change.

*　　*　　*　　*　　*

I once was praying with a woman for inner healing. Her children had been taken away from her because of an addiction. She had stolen things and had run up huge credit card debts on most of her family's credit cards. She was having a great deal of trouble forgiving herself. The Holy Spirit revealed she was believing a lie: that God was ashamed of her. When she confessed and repented of agreeing with the enemy and believing the lies, she was able to hear the truth that God was not ashamed of her. This revelation set her free to accept His great love and choose to forgive herself. Our God stands ready to work out the most difficult situations. Jesus said, "You shall know the truth, and the truth shall make you free" (John 8:32).

Walk in your identity as a beloved, forgiven son or daughter, so that you can give God's love away to others. You will have trouble asking others to forgive and move on if you don't know firsthand how it works.

Sometimes I forget that I am the beloved, forgiven daughter of my heavenly Father. I get overwhelmed and feel inadequate. This is when I say, "Daddy, please remind me who you say I am." Hearing Him tell you that you are beloved is powerful. You can ask the Holy Spirit to fill you again with His love, joy, peace, patience, kindness, goodness, and self-control. Then you can freely pour out this great love and acceptance on others.

Authority Comes from Identity

Jesus has authority over all things: "Then he went down to Capernaum, a town in Galilee, and on the Sabbath he taught the people. They were amazed at his teaching, because his words had authority" (Luke 4:31–32, NIV).

He has given us this same authority to walk in, but we can't do it unless we know our identity in Him. The key to operating in Jesus' authority is an ongoing, close relationship with Him: "Very truly I tell you, whoever believes in me will do the works I have been doing, and they will do even *greater things* than these, because I am going to the Father" (John 14:12, NIV, emphasis mine).

Before my dad died, I was given power of attorney to transact any business as if he were doing it himself. I paid his bills, handled his estate, and generally used this power of attorney as authority to do business as if I were my father. Jesus has given us similar authority over the enemy and his lies when we exercise our authority in His name.

Knowing your own identity and speaking with authority over the lies of the enemy will set both yourself and others free. You become secure in your identity—and authority—as you hide God's Word in your heart. His Word allows you to declare who you are so that you will not fall for the enemy's lies about your inadequacy. You belong to the King of Kings and He will back you up. In Jesus' mighty name, you can cast out demons, heal the sick, and set the captive free. You are a champion for and with Jesus.

The enemy of our souls, Satan, always comes to steal, kill and destroy (see John 10:10). He is into identity theft. He wants to steal your authority as a believer.

You don't have to agree with the enemy's lies. When you do, doubt, fear, and unbelief rise up to undermine your victory in Jesus.

God calls out to you: "Beloved son/daughter, you can do all things through Christ who strengthens you" (see Philippians 4:13). Yes, all things. There are no limits to His strength, His love, His power, His authority. Learn to walk in the authority that you have already been given because, "If God is for us, who can be against us?" (Romans 8:31). That makes you a champion.

Power

The Greek word *dunamis* means dynamic power, great strength, force, capability. It is the same word that gives us our word "dynamite." God's power comes to us from His Holy Spirit. Jesus said: "But you shall receive power [*dunamis*] when the Holy Spirit has come upon you; and you shall be witnesses to Me in Jerusalem, and in all Judea and Samaria, and to the end of the earth" (Acts 1:8). We will discuss this in more depth in chapter 5.

Now power is a gift of the Holy Spirit, but power never validates anyone. We must allow God to cultivate our character as well, or the gifts of the Holy Spirit may get misused. This power is given to those who want to perform signs, wonders, and miracles to the glory of God. Such powerful supernatural manifestations cause people to wonder in awe about who God is and who Jesus really is. When we seek Jesus and allow the Holy Spirit to reveal His power in us, people will come to know Him.

One time out on the inner-city streets, I saw a teen limping along. He had hurt his ankle in a basketball game and seemed to be in a lot of pain. When we approached him for prayer, he said he wasn't religious and wasn't interested. But when I asked him if he wanted the pain to stop, he figured he had nothing to lose. I prayed a simple prayer, "Be healed in Jesus name. Pain leave now." He looked up, grinning. His ankle no longer hurt. He actually put his crutches down and started hopping around.

Delighted, he asked, "How did you do this?" I told him about God's great love for him and how Jesus died for his healing, and on the spot he asked Jesus to take control of his life. When someone is in pain and gets healed, it opens the eyes of their hearts to Jesus. For our part, knowing our identity as champions allows us to approach people, confident that all of heaven is backing us up because of Jesus.

Prayer Power

Some people tell me they don't think anyone has ever prayed for them before. Their families and friends are pre-believers, so they can't imagine who would have ever prayed over them. However, the prayer power of God's champions goes on for eternity. The authority and power of prayers go on beyond a person's lifetime.

I met a young man who was swaggering down the street alone, frowning. He caught my attention as the Lord highlighted him to me. I stopped and said, "May I ask you a question?" and very reluctantly he said, "yes." "What's the best thing that ever happened to you?" He answered, "leaving Chicago, where I almost got killed." We chatted some more and I then asked if I could pray a blessing over him for his safety. As we prayed, the Lord gave me a mental image of an elderly white-haired woman down on her knees by a bed, crying and praying. I told him that his grandma prayed for him and that is why he didn't get killed. This really got his attention.

He said that he used to live with his grandma in Chicago before she died. He loved his grandma very much and missed her. One night, he had been hiding behind a dumpster when someone was shooting at him. When he got home, he passed his grandma's room and saw her on her knees praying. He knew her prayers had saved his life.

Standing there on the street with me, he gave his life to Jesus, all because God had highlighted his grandma's prayers and the power of a praying woman who is now in heaven with Jesus. I know there was great rejoicing in heaven as her prayers for a lost grandson were fulfilled at last.

Our prayers are powerful whether we see them fulfilled in our lifetime or whether they are for future generations. The authority that we have as believers does not expire. There is no time limit on the power in the mighty name of Jesus. It is everlasting.

Overcomers

God was not joking when He said, "I know the plans I have for you . . . plans to prosper you and not to harm you, plans to give you hope and a future" (Jeremiah 29:11, NIV). Against all odds, you are victorious in Jesus. There is a freedom in knowing that you can be yourself. You can blossom into who you were created to be. Once you are free, you will never want to go back to being controlled by what others might think. When our vertical relationship with God is connected, then our horizontal relationships get aligned also.

No longer do you have an orphan spirit. Now you can bring the loving presence of God to the people you meet. You are able to introduce them to your Father so that they, too, can come into the family of God.

Presence evangelism centers around bringing the love of God into hurting or hopeless lives through the tangible or manifest presence of God. You can actually feel it. When we try to do evangelism under our own power, it results in striving and often rejection. People will turn away from a formula or religious words. But when they see the power of God demonstrated in a personal way, they experience God's love and kindness. And it is God's kindness that leads to repentance (see Romans 2:4).

God is all about relationship. He is a loving Father who wants to heal orphan wounds by giving each of His children an intimate family relationship. We were all created for connectedness with the God of the universe through His Son, Jesus, who overcame the power of sin so that we could be true overcomers.

An orphan spirit has nothing to do with having parents or not. An orphan spirit can be found in mature believers struggling with what we call "father wounds" from the past. Father wounds come from performance-based love and they drive our need to be loved and accepted. The orphan spirit causes us to strive for success, compete with each other, act out of jealousy, and define our acceptability by what we can do for God or what others think of us. The fear of failure, rejection, or making a mistake can drive us to avoid reaching out to others.

When father wounds (or mother wounds) get triggered, people withdraw from intimacy with God. The orphan spirit feeds a religious spirit, which becomes a hard, legalistic taskmaster. We become critical and judgmental about the others around us. Sometimes we just give up, because nothing we do ever seems good enough. If you struggle with negative and judgmental thoughts, ask the Holy Spirit to reveal the hidden wounds and convince you of God's love. Let Him help you get the log out of your own eye before you say anything about the splinter in others' (see Matthew 7:3).

It all goes back to knowing your identity in Jesus and walking in the authority of that identity wherever you go. You can't give away what you don't have. You are an overcomer and your assignment is to help turn the hearts of sons and daughters back to their Father.

Why Wouldn't You Tell Me?

I was on the University of Minnesota campus at the end of the school year with a student who wanted to learn how to do "prophetic evangelism." Prophetic evangelism means listening to the Holy Spirit until you sense something from God about a stranger, something that He wants you to tell or ask the person about, and you follow through. Jesus said, "My sheep hear My voice, and I know them, and they follow Me" (John 10:27). Basically, we were practicing being sheep.

We noticed a student with a rainbow-colored, six-inch-high Mohawk hairstyle and many piercings. He really stood out in the crowd. In fact, he attracted so much attention with his looks, I couldn't be sure whether or not it was the Lord who highlighting him. He was talking with a girl so we decided to sit down nearby and wait, writing down what we heard from the

Lord for him in the meantime. My friend was sure her clues would be for him but I wasn't so sure, because my clues didn't seem to fit him.

I was getting prophetic words for someone who really had a teaching gift from God, especially for preschoolers or kindergarten-age children. I felt this person had an anointing to learn languages and also that these gifts were the key to the future. I also felt that the Spirit was saying this person was very creative just like his Daddy God. I did not think my prophetic senses could possibly apply to this rainbow-colored guy. To my mind, they would seem to fit a sweet girl who was nurturing, who loved crafts, and who was majoring in early childhood education.

When we looked up from our praying, he was gone. My friend had been so sure that her clues were for this guy that she almost started crying as the urgency to give away her prophetic words overwhelmed her. We went outside the student center looking for him, and there he was; he wasn't hard to spot. She ran up to him crying with relief to have found him. He calmly and politely said, "Calm down. It's OK. What's the matter?" She explained that we had asked God for prophetic words of knowledge for someone and she thought hers might be for him. He looked skeptical. He told us that he wasn't religious because he was raised in a strict religious family and had left all that behind in his college years.

He was a graduating senior. He had only come back to campus that day to pay a library fine so he could get his diploma. He was moving out of state and would not be back. We would have missed him if we hadn't listened to God. He asked out of curiosity what these words could possibly be.

He asked me first to tell him my prophetic words. I told him that I was looking for someone to whom God had given a passion to teach and encourage kindergarten-age kids, and that God had a plan and a purpose for this person to exceed in an amazing way in the education field. To my eyes he still didn't seem like the right person but now my heart was telling me it was him. I explained how God had anointed this teaching gift to propel him into his destiny. I explained that God said he was creative just like his Daddy God, because the first thing God did was to create. He loved to be creative and kids would really identify and flourish under his teaching.

The student with me asked him if he had a sister and he said "yes, why?" She told him that God had revealed to her that there were some relationship issues and God wanted to mend these and bring family unity. She mentioned that God saw his heart and wanted to heal some abandonment issues, also.

Now, it was his turn to start crying. He told us that he was graduating with a degree in early childhood education and that he loved to teach kindergarten. His parents had died (thus the abandonment issues) and all he had left was a sister, from whom he was estranged. Issues over the inheritance had left hard feelings between them. He was moving out of state to live with her for the summer in hopes of settling these issues before he went abroad, but he was unsure if he was doing the right thing.

He had been hired to teach English to kindergarten students in South Korea (which matched with the anointing to learn languages) and he was wondering if he was equipped to do it. He was so happy that we had heard God affirm his plans of teaching and hopefully reuniting with his sister. He started jumping for joy and praising God even though he had said he was not "religious." He was so excited. We prayed together about his future. We all could feel God's presence and anointing on this creative young man. He could feel it also and commented about the joy and peace he was feeling for the first time in a long time. It was God and he knew it.

Afterward, I told him that I almost didn't share with him as I thought I was wrong. He said, "I plan on taking out the piercings and getting rid of the Mohawk hair over the summer, as South Korea is very conservative." I told him that my hesitancy wasn't about him but about doubting my own ability to hear God correctly. I will never forget the intense words he said next as he looked at me with big tears in his eyes: "Why would you not tell me something that is so life affirming to me? Why would you *not* tell me?"

Knowing that we are God's beloved sons and daughters and that He wants to give us prophetic words for those around us is life-changing—for us and for others. Yes, it's daunting to step out of our comfort zones and risk being wrong. We have to learn to move in our identity, with authority, believing that God wants to talk to us more than we realize. When we are wrong, being secure in our identity will allow us to make mistakes and yet move on. God is bigger than my mistakes. He loves me no matter what I do or don't do, and He wants me to identify with

Him. Identity in Jesus is the catalyst for stepping out of our comfort zone into the amazing supernatural zone.

Application Prayer

Lord, thank you that I am fearfully and wonderfully made. I thank you that you delight in me and that I can celebrate the person I am becoming in Jesus. I agree and declare that you want to talk to me and I want to listen. Give me the boldness of the Holy Spirit that will move me into a supernatural dimension of authority so that, by your power, prisoners can be set free and brokenhearted people can be healed. In Jesus' name, amen.

Chapter 3

Boot Camp Basics

You signed up, now get equipped and trained. Discover how to effectively hear God and move forward in power and authority.

When I was on that mission trip to New Orleans during Mardi Gras that I mentioned in the previous chapter, everyone on our team was supposed to mingle in the crowd, ready to talk with people. Psychics and other occult practitioners had set up their booths and tables on Jackson Square. I had decided that I was all in for sharing with random people, but would leave the witches and warlocks for someone else to approach.

After I shared God's love and prayed with several people, I went to sit on the steps by a girl with a cute puppy. She looked very nonthreatening and we had fun discussing her playful puppy. I soon learned that the girl's name was "Kitten"—and that she read tarot cards, palms, and crystals. She was into witchcraft in a big way, and she had just taken a break from her table to play with her puppy.

I found out that her mother had been a witch and that she was very abusive. This girl had been raised on the streets and had been reading palms and tarot cards since she was eight years old. She mentioned that the only love she had ever really known was from this puppy.

I silently asked the Lord what to say to minister to this hurting and deceived girl. He told me to ask her if she had nightmares, so I did. This young psychic looked surprised and said she couldn't get any sleep, between the puppy and night terrors. I knew that since God had highlighted this, it was something He would use in her life to set her free. I told her that, if she liked, I could ask God to take the nightmares away, because He loved her even more than she loved her puppy. We prayed and a deep peace came over Kitten, the puppy, and me.

Later that evening at chapel, I showed Kitten's picture to the team and asked them to start praying that she would have no more nightmares. We prayed that she would come to know how much God loved her and how much He wanted her to know Him personally.

I went back the next day looking for her but couldn't find her. The following day, I was assigned to a different outreach in another section of the French Quarter. About noon, I started receiving texts from the team members in Jackson Square saying, "Get over here. Kitten is here." When I saw her, she had a long line at her occult table, and the puppy by her side. I waited in line and when it was my turn, she recognized me. We chatted a few minutes and then I asked her if she'd had any more nightmares. Her entire countenance lit up. After our prayer together, she had gotten the first peaceful night's sleep ever. God had taken her nightmares away to show how much he loved her. She was beaming.

God is always speaking if we only choose to listen. He wants to equip us to share His great love with everyone we encounter. Of course it takes practice not to be afraid to step out in faith with what you sense He is saying, but it is so worth it.

In the Bible, Paul (who like the other apostles, practiced this lifestyle) wrote, "Follow the way of love and eagerly desire gifts of the Spirit, especially prophecy. . . . The one who prophesies speaks to people for their strengthening, encouraging and comfort" (1 Corinthians 14:1, 3, NIV).

As we open up to hearing God speak and become willing to sharing His words of encouragement and hope over others, things begin to change. He will always go before us in love. This is one of the primary ways that the prophetic gift has been manifested since Jesus established the Church.

We often think of "prophets" as looking and speaking like Old Testament prophets. In those days, only a few special individuals were considered prophets. But now anybody who belongs to Jesus can be used by the Spirit to prophesy. The book of Revelation says that "the testimony of Jesus is the spirit of prophecy" (Revelation 19:10). Jesus is alive today and desires to communicate with us all. He knows each heart and affirms that we are loved and known by the King of the universe.

As members of His body, we are invited to participate in hearing, knowing, seeing, and sensing what He wants to communicate to us and others. Not everyone is called to the office of prophet but everyone is invited to move in the prophetic gift, to taste and see that the Lord is good as we partner with Him in speaking encouragement, comfort or strength over each other.

Revelation, Interpretation, Application

There are three parts to prophecy: (1) revelation, (2) interpretation, and (3) application.

How does it work? *Revelation* comes when the Holy Spirit gives us words, impressions, pictures, images, "movies," visions, or dreams. He uses our imaginations, Scripture, creative images, dance, angels, circumstances, prophetic happenings, or even a billboard if He chooses. Sometimes we just have "a knowing." He chooses the means to communicate a revelation to you.

Interpretation is usually required before we can share a revelation with others. And it is at this stage that prophecy most often gets off the track. Interpretation is highly subjective. We can go wrong easily because of our own "filters."

The good news is that we are not Old Testament prophets— who were killed when they made a mistake. Today, you can interpret a revelation wrong and you will not get stoned to death.

For example, the word "baseball" may be positive to someone who loves the game and hits the ball well. However, "baseball" may indicate hurt and shame to someone who always the last one picked at recess for the team. You need to become aware of your personal filter and allow the Holy Spirit to heal you where necessary so that God's words can come through His Truth.

Before using it to make tea, I used to rinse out my coffee maker by running water through it several times. My family would always complain because they could still taste the coffee. They are tea-drinkers, not coffee-drinkers, and thus they are sensitive to the taste of coffee. As a coffee-drinker, I couldn't taste the difference. I should have cleaned it better. In the same way, our "filters" need to be cleaned by the power of the Holy Spirit and God's Word.

You can always check your interpretation with someone in authority over you before sharing revelations from God, in particular before giving any directive or warning words. We are to merely deliver the message as it was given to us, without adding our own "extras."

Application is another way of referring to delivering the prophecy—or not. Sometimes we are not supposed to say anything, only to "pray into it." Many times, we will receive a prophetic sense so that we can pray and agree with all of heaven concerning this person or circumstance.

When you have received a timely word that you are supposed to give it to someone, make sure that you are just the mailman delivering the message. You don't need to add to or subtract from what God has shown you.

Words of Knowledge and Words of Wisdom

There is a difference between words of knowledge and words of wisdom. Both are forms of revelation, but only words of knowledge are straight facts. You may receive a word of knowledge about someone's pain or ailment, or a fact such as the person's birth date or a spiritual need. My birthday is March 3 not March 5 or March 7; it's factual and straightforward.

Here is an example of a word of knowledge. I was coming home from a mission trip to Uganda with some friends. We took a short detour for a few days to a healing center in Wales where we had heard reports about miracle healings and supernatural phenomena. This beautiful little retreat center had a very small chapel built on a rock outcropping where legend had it that a monk used to pray over the pagan villagers all day, every day. The chapel only holds about twenty people at the most and they do liturgical readings and worship there.

On this trip, I had been having trouble sleeping because of pain in my left hip due to an old injury. I would toss and turn, trying to get comfortable, and was afraid of disturbing my roommate. During the day, it felt like a nerve was being pinched and it was very uncomfortable. I had been prayed over but nothing had changed, and I was not looking forward to the long plane ride home with a hurting hip.

During worship, a secretary from the office at the Center came over and said she had received a word of knowledge and she hoped it applied to someone so she could get some relief. Her own left hip had started hurting inexplicably. She said, "Does anyone have left hip pain right here?" And she pointed to the exact spot where my pain was. "It feels like a nerve sandwiched between something and it's killing me." I immediately said it was me and asked for prayer. To the great relief of both of us, her pain and mine left immediately and we hugged each other. God had used a clear word of knowledge to heal me.

Practice with friends, family or strangers. You can even say, "Hey, I am practicing getting words of knowledge. Is your birthday March third?" Either you are right or wrong. If you are right, it's encouraging. If you are wrong, you learn to step out humbly in faith and not be afraid of being wrong. (The more powerful lesson is usually learning to survive being wrong.) This may seem like a guessing game at first, but in the long run it may be seriously life-changing for someone.

Words of wisdom involve a revelation about something that is more than just information. A word of wisdom for someone may be that the person has a teaching gift and that God wants to be used for His glory in a powerful way. The person may never have taught before but because of this encouragement, he or she may decide to pursue this gift through further education or by sharing with friends or by leading a Bible study. This kind of affirmation can call into being things that are not. Words of wisdom, coming from the Holy Spirit, release God's desires into our own spirits.

Prophetic Etiquette

In human society, manners and polite rules help us maintain good boundaries in public. You don't pick your nose in public, spit on someone, or push people out of your way rudely. In the prophetic world, we can sum up prophetic etiquette by saying, "Don't give mates or dates or negative prophecies." In other words, "no mates" means don't tell someone whom they are going to marry—such indications and confirmations are reserved for the parties involved. "No dates" because people count on specific information like that, and get very disappointed when it does not happen for whatever reason. This is not a rigid restriction, but rather a strong suggestion so that you can grow in your exercise of the prophetic gift without hurting people.

How do you follow the "no negative words" rule if the word God has given you seems to be negative? For instance, you might sense that someone has a pornography problem. In such cases, I believe we are to call out the person's heavenly identity, not their sin. They know what they are doing but they don't know who they are yet. You might sense the Holy Spirit saying, "Tell him he is meant to be a man of purity who will guard the hearts of women with righteousness." It is life-giving to declare and prophesy as God sees the redeemed person rather than agreeing with his or her sin nature. The Holy Spirit looks at even the pre-believer through the eyes of the loving Father who created him or her. He knows that person's potential, destiny, and calling even when the person is rebelling or running from it.

This is the scriptural approach: "God demonstrates His own love toward us, in that while we were still sinners, Christ died for us" (Romans 5:8).

Let's not agree with the enemy and be an accuser of the brethren but instead let's call out their true identity.

* * * * *

I was with a young man who wanted a haircut before going home to South America. We were out ministering together on the streets, and we decided to stop at a barbershop. Earlier in prayer, I had gotten the word "red shoes." We went to the corner student barber shop and I sat down to wait for him. One of the young barbers sat down by me since he had no customers at the time.

He was wearing bright red shoes. So I told him that he was God's treasure. I asked God for some more words for him and gave him the words. His buddy, a fellow barber student, came and sat down across from us. At first I thought this would distract him from our conversation about Jesus, but instead his friend said, "I have been praying for you for six months, so listen to her."

The fellow in red shoes ended up telling me that he lived alone, he was trying to learn a trade in order to better himself, and that he had never known his dad. The words of prophecy had softened his hard heart to hear and begin to understand that God loved him. He wept as he felt God's Father-heart for him. I led him in praying a salvation prayer and Jesus came into his heart. Just as he finished praying, the receptionist came and said he had a customer. Later he came back. He looked at me and then at his shoes and said, "I haven't worn these shoes in over a year. Do you think God knew this morning that I would pull them out of the back of my closet and decide to wear them?" Yes, God wanted this lonely young man to know that he has a heavenly Dad who cares about him and that what concerns him, concerns Him.

*   *   *   *   *

I was at a strip mall in the inner city where drug dealings are common. I had a young teen with me who hadn't seen his dad in over three years. As we rounded a corner, he looked up and there was his father. At first he wasn't sure, but then his dad called him by his pet name for him. We chatted and then his dad told us, "Y'all get on out of here *now*." He didn't say it in a mean way, but as a warning. We left, but the teen really wanted to go back and pray with his dad. We went out in the parking lot and he met us there. As he held out his hands to pray with us, I sensed the Lord saying that this father was a good businessman, but he was working for the wrong side. He wanted to be a good dad but because he himself had never had a dad, he didn't know how. He nodded his head in agreement. As we prayed, he hugged his son close to him.

I wish that I could report seeing a change in this father, but we are still praying. I believe he will come around; we are believing for his transformation. He heard the prophetic words spoken over him and now it is up to him to decide what he will do.

*   *   *   *   *

Again, prophetic etiquette can be summed up by saying "no mates, no dates, no negative words." Besides eliminating judgmental words, the last part also includes warnings—do not issue prophetic warnings (unless your word has been first submitted to someone in leadership over you).

Last, but not least, do not add the words, "thus saith the Lord." When people hear "thus saith the Lord," they don't feel they have an option to receive or reject your prophecy. They should feel free to disregard your prophetic words without worrying that they are rejecting God Himself. "Thus saith the Lord" also has an overly religious tone that does not work for most people.

Instead, usually it is best to ask very humbly, "Does that make any sense to you?" That gives people an opportunity to receive or reject your word. Remember that you are just the mailman delivering it; you are not responsible for seeing it fulfilled.

It is all right to be brief. When your words are anointed by the Holy Spirit, they will produce fruit. Truly prophetic words are sharp like a sword and they are healing like an ointment poured over wounded hearts for encouragement, comfort, or strengthening.

Application Prayer

Dear Lord, please open the eyes of my heart and open my ears to hear you clearly. Give me an obedient heart to move forward in discerning your words. Activate my prophetic gift so that, like Samuel, I can say, "Speak Lord, for your servant hears you now." May none of my words fall to the ground uselessly but instead reach their God-intended targets with accuracy and anointed power. In Jesus' mighty name, amen.

SECTION 2

Tools

Chapter 4

Contagious Faith

The presence of the Holy Spirit must always be stressed over technique or words. When we learn to hear His voice, we can move out in contagious faith.

By faith, we can choose what we think, and the Bible tells us that as a person thinks, that's the kind of person he or she is (see Proverbs 23:7). Our thoughts determine our actions. As we choose to live by faith and not by sight, a spiritual dimension opens up in which anything is possible. And Jesus said, "With God all things are possible" (Matthew 19:36).

This kind of faith is contagious and the world is desperate for it—desperate for a word of encouragement, strength, or comfort given in faith. When God gives you a word for someone, you don't have to change their circumstances in order to have a positive effect. What you do have is the opportunity to speak life over them. Anointed words from Him are dripping with contagious faith.

Spiritual senses in the invisible supernatural realm are activated by this contagious faith. It is meant to be given away. It is so contagious that if someone even comes near you, they can sense it. The Bible says that even Peter's shadow healed people. You are meant to glow in the dark with contagious faith for a world so in need of restoration and healing.

At times every one of us feels empty. Our faith grows weak and wobbly. That's when we need to catch faith from those around us. Their faith needs to be contagious for us so that our faith can be contagious for the sake of God's work—and for others' faith in turn. It goes round and round.

Right now, is your faith contagious? How can you stir it up to make it stronger? The best ways are by sharing stories about God's wonders and miracles, by reading His Word with enlightenment from the Holy Spirit, and by praising Him in worship.

* * * * *

One time, I had been asked to take a group of young children on an outreach in the inner city. I wanted to encourage them to be creative, so we brought crayons and paper as well as sidewalk chalk. I thought I had heard the Lord say to take the sidewalk chalk to the sidewalk outside a local little group of stores to draw on the pavement and write encouraging words. Where we were headed, drug deals and prostitution are often going on at all hours of the day and night. This may not sound like the safest place to take children, but this is the daily reality of some inner-city neighborhoods.

One little girl had taken a piece of paper and had drawn a picture of a princess with a crown. She excitedly came up to me and pointed to a woman out in the parking lot. "My picture is for her," she said, pointing to a woman in a low-cut blouse and short shorts who was leaning over into a car full of guys.

At first I hesitated. My faith was not as strong as the little girl's was. She "just knew" her picture was meant for that woman, and she had been waiting for just the right person to appear. So, we walked out to the car and I told the woman that the little girl had something for her. The little girl gave her the picture and said so sweetly, "You are a princess and I drew this for you. God told me to tell you He loves you." The woman looked wide-eyed at the girl and then back to the carload of guys. She handed some money back to them and said, "She's right. I am a princess. Y'all get on out of here." As they drove off, we walked back to the sidewalk where we talked, listened, and prayed together, and God touched this woman's heart with contagious love.

Comfort Zone or Carnal Zone?

I used to think that we were supposed to step outside of our "comfort zone." Then one day the Holy Spirit said, "That's not your comfort zone. It's your carnal zone." Instantly I understood that if I could do something by my own strength or my own will, then the thing was within my "carnal zone." I needed to grow in faith so that I could trust Him better. I needed to learn how to step way outside where I felt comfortable in faith.

Each of us must be willing to listen to the Holy Spirit as He leads us in confessing and repenting of fear of man, fear of failure, and striving, as well as doubt about who He says we are. It is a powerful thing to come under conviction of the Holy

Spirit so that we repent of believing the enemy's lies about ourselves. It is truly empowering to be filled and refilled with the Holy Spirit and to welcome Him to lead, guide and propel you into contagious faith adventures.

It takes a lot of faith to step out and risk failure. It takes faith to trust Him to give you a word for someone when initially you have none. Many times, God will highlight someone, and you will think, *There is my next divine appointment. I need to speak to the person, but I haven't a clue what He wants me to say.* It can be awkward at first, but you can always rely on people skills such as smiling, being observant, asking questions, and engaging people in light conversation until you know what He wants you to step out in faith and say.

If you can get over yourself, you can move forward in love. The rewards of seeing people touched and blessed will always far outweigh your own embarrassment. God comes through every time, because He is so faithful. He always backs us up with His love.

* * * * *

Recently, I saw a sales clerk who was busy waiting on people in a long line. People were impatient and some were becoming rude or short with him. When it was my turn, I asked God for an encouraging word for him. He rang up my order and then asked if there was anything else. I was trying not to slow him down even though there was no longer a line. I simply said, "I know this may sound strange but I asked God for an encouraging word for you."

He looked at me wide-eyed, and said, "I have been ostracized by Christians because of my lifestyle choices and I don't think God would want to encourage me."

I asked if I could share what I felt I had heard—simply that the Creator had placed a desire in this man's heart to help people and this desire was sometimes misunderstood. God was affirming that this gift of helps was from Him and he was affirming him as a beloved son. I told him that God knew he loved to help out and that he found great joy in doing acts of kindness for people and for animals. "Does this make any sense?" I asked.

He began to cry. He said he had always been an encourager but felt so misunderstood. He tried to do small acts of kindness and had wanted to start a home for stray animals but he was unsure if he should or not.

I let him know that what he was feeling was the Holy Spirit affirming a God-given gift that was celebrated by the God of the universe who loved him unconditionally. My simple words were heartfelt, because they had been anointed and appointed to draw his attention toward connecting with a God who loved him and who wanted him to dream big to fulfill his destiny.

As he realized that God did know him and better yet wanted a relationship with him, he told me, "Your faith that God wants to encourage me is contagious. I even believe it now."

God's Word

As we read the Bible, God's Word, and hide it in our minds and hearts, it produces a deep well for Him to draw from when we need it most. When we read His Word with revelation from the Holy Spirit, it causes a stirring in our hearts that rejoices, "Yes, He means this and it is true." Psalm 119:11 says, "Your word I have hidden in my heart, that I might not sin against You."

When approaching someone with a word or when praying over someone, Holy Spirit will often highlight a Word from your well. The more you have to draw from, the more He can use it. You don't have to sound religious; even knowing that a revelation comes from the Word of God makes your sharing more powerful.

God wants to develop a personal prophetic language with you. It may include particular pet phrases or pictures. For example, when I see a waterfall over someone's head, I usually think that He wants to refresh him or her. I tell the person, "God loves you just the way you are and couldn't love you any more than He does now. His love is refreshing."

Of course, this isn't a formula, so you should ask Him what He means every time. But you will find that He develops your own special terms of endearment as part of your love language with Him.

Visible and Invisible Realm

We perceive the world around us with our five senses of taste, touch, hearing, seeing, and smell. We can also discern things that are invisible and intangible. These same senses are also real in the spiritual realm.

We can taste and see that the Lord is good—literally. Some things are said to "leave a sweet taste in my mouth" or "leave a bad taste in my mouth."

We might smell an aroma that refreshes us or that triggers memories that carry either good or negative emotions.

Spiritual senses in the invisible realm are activated by our faith; we can choose to live this way, coming into agreement with God as we perceive what He is doing.

Remembering

In order to move forward in faith, God wants us to remember His faithfulness and goodness in the past. We remember that He said He would never leave us or forsake us (see Joshua 1:5), and it builds our faith. We remember what He has done at other times. With that faith, we can step into the spiritual realm and ask for words, pictures, a knowing, a taste, smell, or whatever He wants to give us to help draw people into a relationship with their loving Father and Jesus.

Acknowledge the Visible but Believe the Invisible

Unbelief and lies are often rooted in the visible realm. We may see sickness or some problem and after praying see no improvement. It may be a fact that the person is not getting healed despite our knowing the truth that Jesus died for our healing and the truth that God doesn't want anyone to perish but rather to have eternal life through Jesus. When a person refuses to accept our words and effort, we can become confused. Maybe we got it wrong. Maybe God didn't want to do anything here. That's what seems to be the case, to judge by the visible evidence.

However, in the spiritual realm, where obedience brings blessing; where life is offered instead of death; where love, hope, and joy is the currency of heaven, we can be assured that something *did* happen. Faith chooses to believe that God is faithful, trustworthy, and loving, that He delights in reaching out to His creation.

By choosing to walk by faith and not by sight, we are choosing faith over intellect. Many times, our thoughts are affected by the world around us. It is important to take every thought captive (see 2 Corinthians 10:5) and to choose to allow the Holy Spirit to cleanse our imaginations. Our imaginations were made by God to discern supernatural things. It is a matter of choosing to capture that fleeting "God thought" and focus on it. "For we live by faith, not by sight" (2 Corinthians 5:7, NIV).

You might get just a short, fleeting glimpse of something that God wants to steer you toward. Learn to capture that in your imagination. As you focus on it, you will get more revelation and understanding. The Bible says that we can ask for wisdom and God will give it to us (see James 1:5). While you are waiting, you might get a glimpse of something but not be sure what it means. Searching and asking for more revelation is part of intimacy with Him. By faith we believe He wants to speak to us and reveal secrets of life.

Judging Prophetic Words by Faith

When we get or give a prophetic word, often it sounds nice—but impossible. If the word is sound and it resonates with your spirit, then by faith start "praying into it." For example, if someone tells you prophetically that you have a teaching gift but you have never taught before, start learning what makes a good teacher. Jesus is the best Teacher and He has all the answers. Ask Him to reveal to you what you need to move into your gifting. If you need more knowledge, revelation, wisdom and understanding, ask Him. Knowledge should bring transformation when anointed by the Holy Spirit. By faith, know that you can move forward in this word if it is from Him.

Yet if a word doesn't resonate with your spirit or seems like not the right timing, just put it on the back burner—or flush it.

Your faith should enable you to accept things that you can't even imagine yet. I love the way the Message Bible says it:

> The experts of our day haven't a clue about what this
> eternal plan is. If they had, they wouldn't have killed
> the Master of the God-designed life on a cross. That's
> why we have this Scripture text:
> No one's ever seen or heard anything like this,
> Never so much as imagined anything quite like it—
> What God has arranged for those who love him.
> But you've seen and heard it because God by his
> Spirit has brought it all out into the open before you.
> (1 Corinthians 2:8–9, MSG)

If you are going to encourage others prophetically, then learn to discern the weight of words given. Some are given by trusted and proven prophetic people who can be trusted because of their track record. Others may not seem as formidable but they carry a weight that allows you by faith to appropriate them. When you give someone a word, sometimes you are unsure yourself if it will make any sense to them. Other times, you feel the presence of the Holy Spirit so powerfully that you can't wait to deliver your words.

By faith, believe that God wants to use you to change the world around you for Him. Be bold in love as you step out with words of encouragement, comfort, or strength. By faith, you can have confidence in Him; you know that He will bring it to pass.

Application Prayer

Father, I want to change the world around me for your glory. By faith, I ask you to awaken in me every good gift of creativity, prophetic insight, and boldness in love, attracting pre-believer as well as encouraging fellow believers. Show me what it looks like to make hearing you a priority in my everyday life. Like Samuel, I am listening now. Thank you for increasing my faith. In Jesus' mighty name, amen.

Chapter 5

Plugged In Power

Once we are plugged into the power source, we can give away God's glory. Learn to effectively use the creative tools in your supernatural tool belt to bring honor to Him.

Signs, wonders, and miracles are often the power tools of the Holy Spirit that open doors to present the Gospel. As we learn to love and to listen to the Holy Spirit, we will learn to use the right tools at the right time. We will have confidence to step out of our own comfort zones in faith and engage people. As we get words of knowledge about physical, spiritual, or emotional needs as well words of wisdom about inner healing, we will approach people to ask if they need healing.

One time I was out on the avenue outside the library. I was looking for whomever the Lord would show me, someone whom He wanted to encourage with a word of knowledge or wisdom.

Soon a young couple rode up on bikes and, as they were locking them up, I got a word from the Lord for them. They were both well dressed in clean, nice clothes and the woman's long hair was still wet from the shower. I approached them and engaged them in conversation and then asked if I could share a word with them. The word that I had gotten was that they were homeless and struggling in several areas of their lives. I also thought I might have heard that she was pregnant. But wasn't sure how to go about sharing this word with them as she didn't appear pregnant and they didn't look homeless. I asked the Holy Spirit to open the doors of their hearts to receive encouragement from Him and know He loved them.

As we talked, the man became disinterested and headed off toward the library, but she remained. I asked her if there was anything that I could pray for them. She said that they were struggling financially and had other issues causing friction in their relationship. As we prayed, God's presence came, and she began crying. She said she felt scared and alone as she was facing hard decisions in her life without any guidance. I asked if I could give her a mother's hug and she melted. I told her that God didn't want her homeless and that I thought she might be pregnant.

Now, I usually wouldn't have said that, but felt compelled to let her know that God knew her and this precious baby. She called her boyfriend back from the doorway and told him what I had said. He wanted to know how I knew as they had only found out yesterday that she was pregnant. I told them that their Creator God knew their hearts and had a plan and purpose for their lives as well as this new life. He loved all three of them and would make a way where there seemed none. He said that they had come to the library to look for help either to get an abortion or help in keeping the baby as she wanted this baby. He had been out of prison for just a short time and was having trouble finding a job. He didn't know how he could support a family.

They figured if God put me there to let them know that He knew and cared about this baby, and they said they would look for some help in having this baby.

Later that week, I saw them sitting at a picnic table at a nearby park. I stopped and asked how things were going. They told me they had been able to find some social services and arrange financial help as well as emotional support through a local pro-life crisis pregnancy center. They had been moving from place to place but had felt unsafe in the most recent house, as there were drug dealings going on. The young woman had been able to contact an aunt who took them in when she revealed she was pregnant. Apparently, this aunt just so happened to be a believer and prayer warrior.

They asked if I could pray a blessing over them and this new life. God had used the power of a word to open the doors of their hearts and save this baby and start them on the way to a new spiritual life connection to Jesus.

Power Tools of the Holy Spirit

Jesus said, "You shall receive power when the Holy Spirit has come upon you; and you shall be witnesses to Me in Jerusalem, and in all Judea and Samaria, and to the end of the earth" (Acts 1:8).

He was not talking about just any kind of power living in us as His disciples, but God's supernatural, miracle-working power. We don't have to strive to get this power or to act in it; it is from God Himself. Apart from Him we can do nothing (see John 15:5). All we can do is ask for it and obey whatever He says. He gives this power freely as we ask to be filled with the Holy Spirit. This *dunamis* power is like dynamite in us, and it empowers us to witness about God's great love to others.

The person of the Holy Spirit always points to Jesus, and He enables us to point others to Jesus and His life-giving words (which come to life because of our faith). We are not like the Sadducees, who prided themselves on knowing the Scriptures and yet failed to grasp their significant power. Jesus told them, "Your mistake is that you don't know the Scriptures, and you don't know the power of God" (Matthew 22:29, NLT). Jesus told them they didn't get it. They refused to change or were too stubborn and set in their ways. Meantime their legalistic attitude seduced them to think they were helping God when they defended Him. God does not endorse a religious spirit, and He prefers obedient hearts over defensive ones.

Power Tool: Willing Obedience

Jesus promises us power to witness but we have to ask and then be obedient to the leading of the Holy Spirit—not intent on following our own game plan. The Holy Spirit may give you a Scripture, a word of knowledge or word of wisdom, or a word regarding physical healing or inner healing. However He chooses to do it, the promise is always the same: "You shall receive power when the Holy Spirit has come upon you."

In other words, part of being willing and obedient is taking a risk.

When you sense something, step out in faith even if you are arguing with yourself, "Is that Him or is it just me?" Your being willing to risk attracts the Holy Spirit; when you feel uncomfortable, the Comforter loves to show up! When you are willing to take a risk and trust Him, He always has your back. Your willing, obedient faith in action will bring blessings to others and to yourself. Obedience brings blessings. Period.

Power Tool: God's Word

As I mentioned already, hiding God's Word in your heart gives you another power tool. The Holy Spirit will bring specific Scriptures to your mind to back up what you think He's telling you, and sometimes you can use the very Word of God to declare and decree what He has said, with guaranteed authority and power. Declaring and decreeing God's Word brings transformation to people, places, and entire nations.

Power Tool: Intimacy

Another power tool is intimacy with Him. As we become closer with Jesus and our Daddy God, filled with the Holy Spirit, we can step out in His power. This power comes from your identity as one of His own. It involves hearing His voice and discerning where He is calling you to be at the moment. It's not so much a matter of *doing* as it is of *being*.

We are beloved daughters and sons of the King of the universe. As you become aware of how much He loves you, it gives you the freedom to trust Him in all circumstances, even when you can't see the outcome. This intimacy lets you take down any walls that are guarding your heart and trust Him to guard it.

Lovers get way more done than servants do. He calls you "Beloved." This truth will set you free.

Intimacy with Him will take off the chains that have been hindering you from moving forward. Intimacy with Him propels you from glory to glory (see 2 Corinthians 3:18). No longer will you go five steps forward and then six steps backward; your intimacy with Him keeps you close to Him and above problematic circumstances.

Remember, authority and power are two different things. As a believer, you have authority to call on the name of Jesus in all things. But when you have a close relationship with the One who created you—who knows and loves you and who invites you to know Him—you can tap into His power. He will never fail you. Even if you feel you have failed Him, He will never be disappointed in you. He loves you so much, it's mind-boggling.

*   *   *   *   *

One time, I was in Ukraine with a ministry team. We were told to be ready and prepared on Sunday morning and we would be sent out two by two to preach at different churches. One of the pastors from a little church out in the country was the first to show up asking for a preacher to come back with him. He didn't want just anybody; he asked for our leader. If he couldn't get him, he wanted another man. But he was assigned us two women instead. Gulp. On the ride out to his church, he let us know that he did not believe women should be in ministry.

We both knew we had been called by name and given this assignment. And we knew that because we were beloved daughters, we could count on Jesus not to disappoint anybody. We might be weak but He is always mighty to finish any good work that He has started.

As it turned out, we ended up tag-team prophesying over every single person, young and old, in that church. It was a powerful time, as the manifest presence of God came to these sweet people. They were encouraged, comforted, and strengthened. That day, we saw some healings, both physical and inner healings. We gave God's hope to a couple dealing with infertility. In general, Jesus was there meeting every need. Because of our intimacy with Him, we could move forward in love and power.

By the end of the day, after seeing Jesus' great and visible love demonstrated to his congregation, the pastor changed his mind about "women in ministry" and even invited us to go with him afterward to their meat and cheese shop to pray and prophesy over his wife. I remember telling her that she would soon be copastoring with him and prophesying, too.

She said, "No way! I don't think so."

Needless to say, the next year when we returned, there she was, copastoring and prophesying over their little fellowship. No longer did she feel inadequate, because she had found that she was more than adequate in Him.

Prophetic Intercession

Another power tool is prophetic intercessory prayer. He may give you a word in the night to pray for someone or a city that you don't even know. Prophetic prayer is listening to God and agreeing with Him in prayer that heaven will come to earth in particular people and places.

*   *   *   *   *

Several years ago, before it was even in the news, I heard the word "Aleppo" in my sleep. I knew Aleppo was a city, but when I awoke, I had to look on Google to find out that it was in Syria. I started praying for the people of Aleppo to come to know Jesus, that He would walk down their streets, and that love and peace would fill the place.

When I heard in the news about Aleppo's bombings and war, I knew there was no peace yet. At times, I even felt like maybe I hadn't prayed hard enough as things got worse there. I saw the pictures of a once-beautiful, historic city turned into ruins and death lurking everywhere. I came to understand that I was probably just one of many that He was asking to pray. He wanted a number of us to agree with heaven that the people of Aleppo would come to know Him and His great love for their war-torn city.

I declared and decreed that the children would be able to be set free from post–traumatic stress disorder and come to know the Prince of Peace. I knew that there is power in prayer and agreeing with heaven even when we don't see it manifesting on earth yet.

There is also power in knowing, "I was created to do this." You may feel an unexplainable joy inside as you move in the power of His presence. Other times, you will feel nothing. People sometimes get confused and think that the more powerful gifts of the Spirit are showy and loud. Bu

strength of power manifested in weakness that

Holy Spirit party. It's the still small voice t

yelling does not delight Him. (Stop and thin

you have to yell to get someone's attention, it'   ⌐ ᴜᴄᴄause

they are not paying attention. Pay attention to the Holy Spirit

and move in unity with Him and you won't miss His quiet

instruction.)

How well do you know the person of the Holy Spirit? When you move with Him, not ahead or behind, but in rhythm and flow with Him, there is power. It's like slow-dancing with a beloved spouse with whom you can move as though you are one.

Knowing the Times and Seasons

We need to understand the seasons and timing of the Spirit. Different seasons call for different tools and plans, and any given undertaking requires ongoing sensitivity to the Holy Spirit for carrying out God's plan.

Think of the seasons of the natural year. You may use a tiller in the spring to plow up and plant your garden. In summer, you may use a hoe to remove weeds. However, in the fall when you harvest a crop or rake leaves, you use different tools. You don't use a snow blower to plow in spring. You have to put away perfectly good tools in one season in order to be in sync in another. If your hands are full because you haven't put down the old (but good) tools, it's hard to grasp new ones.

he same way, you need to be aware of both the current
tual season and the power tools that are being called for, as
the Spirit leads. If you rely on a formula or how God moved in
the past, you may miss it. He is always creating. Although He is
the same yesterday, today, and forever, His strategies change.

*   *   *   *   *

I was praying for our local high school to see revival and for
the students to come to know Jesus personally. In my spirit, I
could see the word "strategy" over the building in neon letters. I
thought God was going to give my team a strategy to enable us
to take this high school for Him. Instead, each week as we
faithfully went to the school, first prayer walking around it and
then being invited into the halls after school to pray, each week
was different. We had to ask God what He was doing and get on
board with Him with new tools for that week.

On the first week, we just happened by divine appointment
to meet a teacher who had been asking God for students to start
praying and meeting in her room. We started meeting there
every week. Soon, we had a few students coming who were very
shy. The school rules specified that school clubs had to be
student-led to be allowed to function at the school. These
students stepped out way beyond their comfort zones to be the
leaders in our after-school club. This club is still ongoing, and we
are looking for what God has in store for the students of our
local high school.

Kindness and Generosity

Kindness and generosity can work together as a power tool for God's work, because giving gifts opens hearts to the Giver. In our inner-city ministry, we give away food, provide community cookouts, and perform acts of service such as clearing snow from sidewalks or picking up trash (while prayer-walking the neighborhood), and many other services. As we have prayed over this inner-city neighborhood, we have seen lives and streets transformed. Many times the acts of kindness have softened people's hearts to receive powerful life-changing prayer that leads to salvation, healings, and freedom.

* * * * *

Godtown is the name of the movement and community in the inner city where we all worship and serve together, but attend our own churches. We find that there is power in living in community with like-minded believers.

One time, I was leading a group of Godtown people on an outreach. As we were prayer-walking and blessing the neighborhood, we saw a sign: "Keys to Paradise." It was in front of an occult book store that sold potions, New Age paraphernalia, and such. A witch's broom was secured over the door inside and many occult potions and items were on the walls and shelves. Our group went in to greet them, saying we were neighbors and wanted to bless them. We were thinking about how you can bless people with the gift of coming to know God's great love for them and power of Holy Spirit setting them free.

The store clerk was a young lady who had a little baby. Numerology was her religion. She wanted us to pray for her baby, which we did, and later we brought her some baby clothes. This turned into a good relationship. Eventually the store shut down and we now rent this space ourselves. It's now called Freedom Center, and classes take place every day to help build relationships—our vertical relationship with God and our horizontal one with others. We host deliverance classes, inner healing sessions, Narcotics Anonymous meetings, Alpha and Teen Alpha sessions in summer, Yo Yo (a group for teens), and a community food giveaway from this site.

Initially, when children would come in they would ask, "Is this a haunted house?" They could sense the evil spirits leaving. As the new renters, we worshipped and proclaimed the blood of Jesus over every inch of that place, standing in our heavenly authority to command the spirits to leave in Jesus' mighty name.

Many people have been set free by the power of God in this Freedom Center. People have come looking for potions or help in getting evil spirits out of their houses and they have met the Lord as we have prayed with them. It all started as an act of kindness toward the people involved with this occult place.

On a side note, there are apartments above this rental space. One day I happened to see a young Hmong man leaving one of the apartments and going to his car. I asked him if he could tell the difference since the old renters had left and we moved in. I also mentioned that I hoped the praise music and singing wasn't too loud. He told me that they loved the praise music, as they were Catholic believers. He also said that his appliances—

toasters, microwaves, and the like—used to break on a frequent basis when the other renters were downstairs, and that nothing broke down anymore since Godtown had taken over the space below his apartment.

All this came from using the power tool of kindness and generosity.

The Word of Your Testimony

The power of your own testimony is another power tool in your tool belt. By "your testimony" I mean your unique, personal story of being set free and empowered by God's Spirit. Oftentimes, we find that we are drawn unconsciously to people who have similar issues to the ones that tripped us up. When we have been set free from something, we become overcomers, with particular authority over those specific issues and spirits. We also have greater compassion for someone who is struggled as we once did, and we know how it feels to be set free.

Personally, my husband and I have struggled with infertility; I had five miscarriages. We are now blessed with four healthy adult kids, three "sons-in-love," one adorable grandbaby and more on the way, and many beloved spiritual sons and daughters, but I still find that I often pray over women who are struggling to get pregnant. From the inside, I know the heartache, depression, and loss of hope. I also understand how some people are infertile in the spirit, not only physically. I know that they are called to give birth to something spiritually that will lead to life and blessing for others, and that this birthing may need to be protected from miscarriage or stillbirth. I used to work as a nurse, and when I worked in women's health I could often pray over women who had been defeated by infertility and miscarriages. It was the power of my personal testimony that allowed God to break through others' defeats. He turns our mourning into dancing (see Psalm 30:11) and moves us forward in love and faith.

No one can argue with your personal testimony. It is unique to you and part of your life story. Sometimes I ask people, "What is the best thing that ever happened to you?" I listen first to their story and then ask permission to tell them the best thing that has ever happened to me. I use a great tool called the "One-Minute Testimony." I have practiced giving my testimony in just one minute, in three parts: First, what was my life like before Jesus? Next, what changed? And last, how did that affect me?

Once you know how to give your testimony in a concise manner, you can count on the Holy Spirit to use it to bring people to know Jesus.

The Most Powerful Tool

One power tool is the best of all: love.

Love covers a multitude of sins. Love never gives up. A 1 Corinthians 13 kind of love is unconditional and is born of the Father's great love for us in giving His only Son for our salvation. Love, love and more love is undeniable. It allows us all to rise to new life.

If you approach people with anything but love, the Bible says you sound like a noisy gong, annoying and irritating to others (see 1 Corinthians 13:1).

Love makes a way when there appears to be none. Love moves in power to overcome even the most stubborn of hearts. Even if you are rejected, love still wins. If nothing else, people can tell when love is being expressed, just as they can also discern unspoken judgmentalism or criticism. Love draws people; they feel accepted and safe.

God's love has the power to transform hearts and lives, and it can set people free. We see it expressed by Jesus when he read from Isaiah 61 in the synagogue in Nazareth:

> The Spirit of the Lord is upon Me, because He has
> anointed Me to preach the gospel to the poor; He has
> sent Me to heal the brokenhearted, to proclaim liberty
> to the captives and recovery of sight to the blind, to
> set at liberty those who are oppressed; to proclaim the
> acceptable year of the Lord. (Luke 4:18–19)

Part of the power of love is choosing to forgive. When we choose to forgive others and ourselves, it sets us free to love in power. Through a single act of forgiveness, people sometimes get set free of addictions or healed or delivered of evil spirits in a miraculous instant. Other times, it is a longer process, getting set free and falling back and then getting set free again. Love always wins through. Love always hopes and believes the best. Love never fails, nor does it keep account of wrongs. Forgiveness does not mean that we "enable" others; we must use wisdom and maintain good personal boundaries.

The power tool of love is so important because it is the basis for all we do. As we choose to confess, repent, and ask for forgiveness for ourselves, we can be filled up over and over to full and overflowing. When you are full it is only natural to overflow on all around you with no effort. When you come back to our first priority—putting Jesus first—everything else will fall into place as you are willing and obedient. You will be ready for anything. He will set you up with divine appointments daily so you can let the Father's heart for people be revealed through yours.

Sometimes, I get a word of knowledge that makes my heart feel as if it is on fire. It happens often when I encounter the disenfranchised of this world, the outcasts of society who have lost hope. They are so precious to our Father even before they seek Him. When I get this "heartburn," I ask God to show me the person's real identity and hidden destiny so that I can call out the gold that is in them. I never need to mention the dirt of the world that is apparent on them. Eyes of love look past it.

Love is powerful because it shows someone their identity as a beloved son or daughter of the King of the universe. God's great love demonstrated through Jesus and empowered by the Holy Spirit bring us all into the family of God. Love builds Kingdom family in a powerful way.

Application Prayer

Dear Lord, show me how to love as you do. Fill me up to overflowing. Thank you that you want to give me every good gift and not withhold any good thing. Walking in your power and authority, I want to bring others into your Kingdom family. Show me how to use the power tools you have created to change the world, one person at a time. In Jesus' mighty name, amen.

Chapter 6

Viral Compassion

Jesus' compassion was His motivation for engaging people.
Life experiences have left people needing to encounter love
and compassion. Is your compassion contagious?

One time I took a youth group from a local church out on
the streets on a treasure hunt. They weren't sure they
even wanted to be there, let alone step out and use the gifts of
the Spirit. One girl stated that she was only there because her
mother had put her in this particular youth group while she was
at work so she could have a good place to make new friends and
pass the time under supervision. She let me know that
witnessing was not on her agenda for the summer and that she
certainly didn't know how to heal anyone.

I liked this girl right from the get-go. She was open and
honest and she had a compassionate heart. I felt that God was
going to use her to empower the rest of the group.

I explained how we were going to go out on the streets
looking for clues that God was going to give us, how we were on
a treasure hunt because people are God's treasures. She spoke
up and said, "I don't think I can hear from God, so how will this
ever work?" Probably she was speaking for the whole group, but

everyone else kept their reactions to themselves and didn't speak up.

I understood where they were coming from, as I had often felt the same way. But thank goodness we have a God who is so much bigger and more powerful than our own insecurities. I simply told them that they were His sheep and His sheep *will* hear His voice (see John 10:27). I mentioned that God's voice is speaking all the time just like a radio broadcast, but you need to be on the right channel. He wants to speak to your heart even more than you want to hear Him.

With this in mind, we prayed and then listened. They wrote down clues that they thought they might be sensing in the Spirit. As we shared clues about locations, articles of clothing, names, unique issues, they began to get excited. Several kids got the same two clues: "red baseball cap" and "bus stop." One of them felt that we would encounter someone who had a broken leg that was in a cast. Another said it would have something to do with a motorcycle.

Based on their clues, we set out for the local bus stop looking for people to pray for. We went in groups of three so as not to overpower people. I was one of a threesome with the outspoken girl. We went to the bus stop but didn't see anyone. The rest of the group went on across the street to look for their clues. As we waited, the bus came and a young man wearing a faded red baseball cap with a leg cast and crutches stepped clumsily off the bus. He was having difficulty and seemed to be in a lot of pain, to judge by the grimace on his face. He came over to sit down on the bench, looking exhausted. We approached him and asked him about his cast and leg. He had been in a recent motorcycle accident and had broken his leg. He was still in a lot of pain and the crutches were hurting his underarms, too.

The young man told us that his pain level was 12 on a scale of 1 to 10. We asked if we could pray for the pain to leave and he accepted this offer. After getting his permission, I asked the reluctant girl to just put her hand on the cast and say, "In Jesus' name, be healed. Pain, leave now in Jesus' name." She did.

He started grinning and said he thought all of the pain had left after she prayed. "How did she do that?!" he asked. The girl was as surprised as he was, and they both started shouting for joy. We were able to tell him that we had approached him because God had revealed clues to us. We told him that he was God's beloved son and that God wanted to have a relationship with him. Now that his leg was pain-free, his heart was open to meeting this Jesus who loved him enough to send someone to pray for his pain to leave.

There usually is more to the story, and in his case there was more. His father was a pastor and this prodigal son had been hurt by the church's treatment of his parents, so he had been running from God. God had called him, but "sheep bites" had wounded him and kept him from saying yes to God. (Sheep bites happen when people in a church—the "flock"—gossip, slander, and hurt each other or their pastors, or shepherds, who take care of them.)

This reluctant young girl's entire demeanor changed. She was reluctant no more. She had stepped out in faith and God had used her to heal someone physically and spiritually. Her compassion for this hurting young man caused her to "go viral" with her faith. She ran across the street to tell her friends what had happened.

What Is Compassion?

In the previous chapter we talked about the power of love. How does compassion fit into the picture? Compassion is a loving response to the suffering of others. It is highly motivating. Compassion causes someone to go out of the way to help out.

Jesus was motivated by compassion whenever He reached out to people. Compassion caused Him to heal them, feed them, and set them free. His compassion was obvious when He raised the widow's son from the dead (see Luke 7:11–17) and also when He raised Lazarus from the dead. The story portrays it: "Jesus wept. Then the Jews said, "See how He loved him!" (John 11:35–36). Jesus' compassion compelled Him to "stop for the one" as He looked for lost individuals who were outcasts.

Jesus' compassion is what motivates us to move outside what we would be comfortable doing normally. When that compassion goes viral, we want the whole world to know that God loves them. Compassion moves us to seek out the lost, hurting, and seemingly forgotten people we meet.

In treasure hunts such as the ones I have been describing, the clues God gives us allow us to participate in feeling God's heart of compassion for others. It's like going out with a bow and arrow, looking for the one person who is the target of God's clues. Other times we may go out with more of a shotgun approach, speaking to anyone who is living and breathing. Both kinds of treasure hunts work only when they are handled with love and compassion.

Every pre-believer can be ready, but not every pre-believer is ready. Life experiences have left people needing to encounter love and compassion. Compassion makes us creative in how we witness to people. Let me tell you about some ideas we have tried.

Balloons of Hope

One time we went out on the university campus with helium balloons. We had written on the balloons, "Encouraging words here" with arrows pointing down toward us. Students jostled by us and really didn't seem interested at all. That is, until a student in a wheelchair rolled up to us and asked what our balloons meant. She said that she would love any encouraging words as she was overwhelmed by her life at present. We were able to pray with her and lead her to the Lord with encouraging words and compassion for her feelings of inadequacy. We also prayed for her physical healing, but it was her hurting heart that most needed to feel the compassion of the Lord through us.

Prophetic Pictures

Another time, I collected random photos of different places and things and told my team to write prophetic words on them to give to people. I instructed team members to ask God for encouraging, strengthening, or comforting words to write on the backs of the pictures. For example, on the back of a picture of a sprouting seed, one of them wrote something about new life coming forth and a new season coming.

We took our pictures and headed out to the local state fairground where we knew there would be crowds and where people would be handing out all kinds of things already.

One of our girls had five pictures and she asked a man to choose one as she fanned them out like cards in her hand. He chose one, read it, and handed it back to her, saying, "This doesn't apply to me and I will only throw it away," he said. This particular girl struggles with rejection and wanted to go home after this. The rejection of her picture seemed to confirm to her what she already thought about this whole venture. (She had told me her words were "stupid" and wouldn't encourage anyone.) However, because she loves children, she had compassion for a little girl who wanted her mommy to choose a picture. So, she fanned out the photos again and the woman picked the same one the man had rejected.

My young teammate was trembling as she waited for the woman to reject the picture too. However, the mother read it and started crying as she called her husband over. She explained that her husband had lost his job and they were struggling financially. Her neighbor had given them tickets to the fair to cheer them up and encourage them. She looked at the picture of the new growth of springtime and read on the back: "God sees your struggles and wants to give you a new season of hope and change for the good. He is encouraging you that He loves you and has a plan and purpose for your future. Jeremiah 29:11. He loves you so much."

The same one the man had rejected meant so much to this little mama and her family. The compassion of the girl had compelled her to risk rejection again and offer her photos that she didn't think were very profound. Simple words given with compassion carry a powerful anointing of God's love. We prayed and blessed this sweet little family as they went into the fair, encouraged that God would provide. Viral compassion had touched their hearts.

Tattoos and Jesus

I love the way God blends and uses the zeal of the younger generation and the wisdom from those who have lived longer, made more mistakes, and (we hope) learned from them. One time, a beautiful white-haired woman joined us. She was very eager to learn to share her faith but our plan that day gave her pause. That particular day we were going to visit men at a homeless mission where we would look for tattoos and interpret them as prophetic signs.

She shared that she had been raised in a very religious family with strong feelings that tattoos are not appropriate. Furthermore, for her tattoos only triggered the thoughts of a broken relationship with her rebellious son who had left their family with much heartache and broken promises.

I have friends who own a tattoo parlor and they are passionate believers. I have prayed over their tattoo parlor and for them many times and I consider them to be very creative and talented. I had asked if I could use pictures of some of their beautiful and creative tattoos to practice interpretation with the group. This whole thing was way outside this woman's comfort zone. However, she went ahead and participated in the exercise because she realized that this could open up a new way to communicate with her prodigal son.

Later, really mostly out of compassion for her son, she approached several young men and shared a mother's love as she told them her testimony. She was powerful out on the streets that day. Not only did she have a personal breakthrough but so did several of the young men at the homeless mission we visited.

Creative Compassion

The first thing our Daddy God did was to create the world and all that is in it. He is still creating. We are just like our Father—love compels us to be creative. God's love and compassion flowing through our hearts can also enable us to try new things. Even people who do not consider themselves creative can try to paint or do something artistic.

For this reason, we have set ourselves up in public gatherings to offer prophetic face painting, free spiritual readings, dream interpretation, and other innovative ways to engage people with God's love.

Dream Interpretation

Everyone has dreams, even if they can't remember them. The Bible is a great dream interpretation book because it's full of meaningful symbolism and examples of dream interpretation. When I see how many people seek dream interpretation in the wrong places, I want to study dream interpretation even more in order to share God's love.

Have you ever had a dream or nightmare that you didn't understand and no one could help you interpret? It makes you appreciate the power of Holy-Spirit-guided dream interpretation. Often God is communicating with people through their dreams and we have the honor of helping them get revelation from Him.

Speaking for the Lord, the Old Testament prophet Joel said, "I will pour out my Spirit upon all people. Your sons and daughters will prophesy. Your old men will dream dreams, and your young men will see visions" (Joel 2:28, NLT). This happened on the day of Pentecost when the Holy Spirit was poured out on the believers. Since then, God speaks through dreams not only to "old men," but to everybody.

In the Bible (see Judges 7), we read about Gideon, who was supposed to lead the troops into battle, but who needed encouragement ahead of time that he was going to win before he would risk his life and others' lives. He was hesitant until God told him to go sneak down into the enemy camp where he would overhear someone talking about a dream. Listening to a stranger interpreting a dream made it possible for him to go out and fight successfully.

If God could use the dreams of an enemy to encourage this man, how much more can He give guidance through dreams to those who are seeking Him? God loves to reveal our destiny to us, whether in the day or at night. He is there for us 24/7, always communicating. Sometimes it is easier for him to communicate with us when the business of the day is out of the way and we are no longer preoccupied with other things. In sleep, He has our full attention.

In order to keep track of your dreams, you must keep paper and pen by your bed to write them down as soon as you wake up. Dreams seem to leave our memory otherwise. Besides, it can be helpful and interesting to look back over your recorded dreams to see the connections with your life as it unfolds.

Some dreams are not so fleeting. You may have reoccuring dreams because God is telling you something several times until you get it. You may have a dream that seems to disturb you or beg for an interpretation. God wants you to draw closer to Him for revelation.

He is the One who gives both the dream and the interpretation. Seek wise and trusted counseling on dream interpretation and ask the Holy Spirit for revelation. The interpretation should resonate with your spirit, give you a deeper understanding of His great love for you, or give you positive direction and affirmation. If it is a cleansing dream, you can take comfort in knowing that as you agree with Him, He will set you free in a special way.

I have had the honor of teaching dream interpretation classes and heard a lot of dreams. One young man told me, "I never dream." He was very adamant about this. Everyone in the class started sharing their dreams and he always enjoyed helping figure out the interpretations. However, he always stated, "I don't dream and don't want to, either." As time went on, people kept encouraging him to be open to dreaming and they prayed over him to dream. Eventually, he revealed that he'd had several reoccurring nightmares as a child and he had become afraid to go to sleep. He had made a pact with himself that he would never dream again. In other words, out of fear he had word-cursed himself. Thankfully, curses can be broken. This young man realized that he had believed the lie that if he didn't dream, all fear would leave him. The truth that he could trust God with his days and nights has set him free to dream.

Dreams are a blessing meant to encourage you and give revelation about how much God cares for you and your everyday life. He wants to direct you, give you warning or just encourage you that things will be all right. He also uses dreams to give you ideas, help you make decisions, and share with you plans for inventions. You may be struggling with a major decision and get clarity about it through a dream.

Dreams are just as significant an avenue for God's communication today as they were in the past. You may hear about New Agers or others who say they can interpret dreams but the real interpretation must be God-given. Dream interpretations, like other messages from God, must convey His heart of love and compassion, not personal opinions or judgments or fads.

*   *   *   *   *

While on a mission trip to Philippines, I was part of a group that set up a carnival in a park. We divided ourselves up to organize various activities: face painting, prophetic pictures hanging on a clothesline, a band, testimonies, and dream interpretations. This event had several different mission groups working together in beautiful unity, but one of the missionaries—who thought dream interpretation was "New Age" and who found it far outside his comfort zone—brought over a young man from the slums of Manila to get a reoccurring dream interpreted. This young man had been on the streets in the slum all his life and had robbed and stolen to survive. He was a new believer who was being discipled by this missionary, but he was troubled by this reoccurring dream.

In his dream, his teeth were always falling out. He would be dismayed at first, but he always got new and improved teeth. I simply shared that I thought God wanted to give him an entirely new group of good and trustworthy friends and that this would change his life in such a dramatic way that he would be able to taste and see (with his new "teeth") that God is good. I didn't know his background at the time nor did I know about a big decision he was trying to make. The missionary told me later that this teen had the opportunity to leave the slum, join Youth With A Mission and live elsewhere. He would make all new friends but was afraid he wouldn't fit in and didn't know how he would raise financial support.

As he was raising support, his missionary friend emailed me again. This teen didn't speak or write English but he remembered the dream interpretation that had given him the courage to move forward. He wanted to know if I could help support him as he didn't know anyone outside the slum. Compelled by compassion for him, it was an honor to sow into this young teen's future. (Sometimes, reaching out with compassion will literally cost you something, but what a joy it is to be a part of someone's transformation.) Because of that dream interpretation, he applied, got accepted, and moved. He went on his first mission trip and did an excellent job.

*　*　*　*　*

One of our Godtown urban missionaries used to tell me that she didn't hear from God prophetically. However, she had a lot of dreams. In fact, she had epic dreams that were like movies. We started doing dream interpretation, which she loved and was good at. Learning to interpret her dreams showed her that God really did want to speak to her. Eventually, she began to realize that she could also hear God in other ways.

She has a heart and compassion for missions and God was speaking to her about her destiny.

One time she had a dream that she should go to Mongolia on a short-term mission trip. She didn't know anyone in Mongolia but, propelled by her dream, she investigated missions there. She discovered that there was a German group working in Mongolia and that they had a base in Texas. She raised support and went to explore possibilities and get to know the Texas group. Eventually, she did a long mission trip to Mongolia and fell in love with the people there. All of this happened because of a dream; she heard God and was obedient.

*　*　*　*　*

Sometimes compassion compels you to do something that later makes you question if you really heard from God or not.

On one particular outreach, I had gotten the clue, "conductor's hat." We were downtown in St. Paul, Minnesota, so I walked to the Union train station, but found no conductors. Then I thought maybe it would be a bellhop's hat so went to the St. Paul Hotel to look for the person. I ended up just sharing with random people as I never found anybody with a conductor's hat. I went home and forgot about it.

The next day, my daughters were in town and we went to walk around a lake together. We noticed a trolley close by and we decided to ride on it. I had never ridden it before that day and I have never ridden it since. As we walked toward the trolley, which had three conductors, I was excited to be with my visiting daughters and wasn't thinking about conductor hats anymore.

However, one of my daughters reminded me of my clue. So I picked one of the conductors and simply started chatting with him. I told him I had been looking for someone wearing a conductor's hat. I eventually asked if I could pray a blessing over him. I told him that he was God's treasure, and he asked, "Exactly what do you mean by that?" Then I started getting words for him along the lines that God was already intervening in his finances and that he didn't need to worry. Every word was about his finances, and all of them were very positive. He was dumbfounded, and he explained why.

He said that God had given him a heart of compassion for the inner city. He used to be a senior pastor in a suburban church and he and his wife had a comfortable life. He had left the church, full of compassion and enthusiasm, to start an inner-city ministry. But now they had drained their savings. Finances had dried up and they were several months behind on their mortgage payments. He was questioning if he had heard God correctly.

But God had sent him encouragement through me and my daughters. We ended up taking pictures together, laughing with joy. His compassion for the inner city had caused him to make a big life change and now God was affirming his decision. We were sure that He would meet every need of our new friend.

"Feelers"

We can't talk about viral compassion without talking about people who are "feelers." This is what we call people who have so much compassion in their hearts that they can actually feel other people's pain, depression, or other emotions. If you know what I'm talking about, perhaps you are a feeler yourself. If so, ask the Holy Spirit to transform your gift, suffusing it with his powerful compassion. You don't want to be weighed down by all of the negative feelings you pick up on. You are meant to be an atmosphere-changer instead of letting the atmosphere change you. You are supposed to be a thermostat, not a thermometer.

Have you ever walked into a room full of people and you could feel the depression? Many feelers get uncomfortable in a crowd because they are bombarded by unwelcome emotions. You need to learn what to do with this emotional information. You are not meant to be jerked around by emotions—your own or others'—because feelings make lousy guides.

To put it in the language of Scripture, you are meant to be the head, not the tail: "The Lord will make you the head and not the tail; you shall be above only, and not be beneath, if you heed the commandments of the Lord your God" (Deuteronomy 28:13).

You can walk into a crowded room with God's wisdom and compassion guiding your emotions. Then you can speak life, health, and blessing over the place and the people around you.

Your words of declaration are powerful. God's economy is a spoken one. He spoke the universe into being. Jesus is known as the Living Word.

When you speak words of life over brokenhearted people, hope gets restored and faith rises up. This can apply even to people who are so overwhelmed by their negative emotions that they are suicidal. God's transforming, restorative love is stronger than generational depression, sexual trauma, abandonment, addictions, and a host of other serious mental and emotional issues. In fact, only God can truly set prisoners free from destructive thought patterns and enable them to hear His voice of love.

It all works because of His compassion. When His great love—expressed through one of us who comes in His name—touches a person or place, the atmosphere changes. Love is in the room. Hope and joy rise up to meet Him. All we have to do is release our Spirit-breathed compassion wherever we go, and we will see God's Kingdom coming to earth before our eyes.

Application Prayer

Dear Lord, please take my emotions and use them to compel me with your compassion for others. Show me what that looks like on a daily basis. Bring any emotions not planted by you under the control of the Holy Spirit. I give you permission to cause me to laugh at what makes you laugh and cry with what breaks your heart. In Jesus' name, amen.

Chapter 7

Prophetic Workout

People wonder, "Is that just me or is that God?" As we practice listening to God and as we obediently speak His encouraging words, our faith soars and our prophetic muscles grow.

Sometimes we can hear God clearly and we can follow Him obediently. Other times, we are not sure. Nothing is clear; God's voice seems faint and vague. We wonder, *Is God speaking to me or is that just my own thoughts?* We wish we had a guaranteed method to follow, because it would be so much easier for us.

The truth is that we can never expect to have a method or formula to follow—because we are following Someone, not something. It is a *relationship,* and it grows and changes as we communicate with God Himself. As we walk with Him, we learn to recognize His voice, whether He speaks loudly or softly. We learn from our mistakes. We love Him as He loves us.

Even when we have an experience with God in which His voice is loud and clear, our hearing is based on our ongoing relationship with Him. Think about what happened with Peter when he was summoned to Cornelius' house (see Acts 10). Peter needed a clear word because God was telling him to do something that contradicted his Jewish training. He even protested, "But Lord, I have never eaten anything unclean. . . ." Yet he trusted God so much that he overcame his internal objections and obeyed the Spirit's command, traveling to the Gentile Cornelius' house and preaching the Gospel, whereupon all of his listeners were not only saved but also baptized in the Holy Spirit and in water. His obedience released the message that God's salvation was meant for non-Jews.

In any relationship, we have to learn to take risk. We may get hurt. But the more we learn from our ongoing relationship, the better we get at picking up subtle clues about the other person. In the case of our relationship with God, the better we get at discerning His often-quiet advice.

I love working with young adults. Most of them are single and they don't want to be single forever. Sometimes they ask me how I knew my husband was the right one. (I am very blessed to have been married to a wonderful man of God for over forty-three years.) I can tell them my story, but I can't tell them how to fall in love. I can teach them relational skills, pray for inner healing, and affirm their identity, but each individual has to discover his or her own life partner. I can give advice about character and integrity but only God knows the true intentions of the human heart.

God desires people of all ages, all nations and all generations to know Him actively. It's not just about a salvation prayer but making a relationship with Him a daily priority.

Learning to Discern His Voice

The more we practice hearing God and then being obedient to what He has impressed on our hearts, the more our discernment "muscle" grows. Knowledge is only transformational when it is followed by action.

The reason we practice hearing God and being obedient in spite of risks is to reveal God's heart of love to people. When people realize that the God of the universe *knows* them and loves them, they become open to inviting Jesus to become their Savior and Lord.

There have been many times when God has put someone on my heart for just a fleeting moment. It may be someone I haven't thought of in years, and I dismiss it. Later, I find out that something was going on and that brief thought was meant to alert me to pray for or contact the person. I have learned by my mistakes that God is intentionally random. When I get a fleeting thought, I can ask if it is from Him. I then can ask the Holy Spirit what He wants me to do. Should I simply pray in secret, send an encouraging email that says, "God put you on my heart," or wait for more specific instructions? It is a great joy to grow in hearing God and being obedient to Him in this way.

* * * * *

Our area of the country has a large population of Hmong people who came as refugees from southeast Asia mountain regions—a people with no country. At a summer teen Hmong camp called Shekinah Camp I was asked to teach a short, hour-long class about how to hear God prophetically.

I didn't know how much they understood about hearing God and prophecy. As I asked Him for revelation and wisdom for the class, I felt it should be a very interactive time. ("What do you see . . . sense . . . hear? What do you think it means?") I taught for about twenty minutes and then we played prophetic games. These kids were hungry for God and they had an awareness of the spiritual realm that other teens in our Western culture do not. They went from 0 mph to 100 mph in a very short time. We were all laughing, hugging and feeling God's presence in a powerful way.

Most of these kids had been raised in a culture where the spirit world is real and God's written Word is honored. They just needed to be affirmed regarding what they already knew and they could be off and running. They had already cultivated a relationship with God, and it made sense to them to constantly ask for words of wisdom, revelation, discernment, knowledge, correction, or whatever was needed.

Prophetic Workouts

Most people tend either to be unsure of themselves, so they withhold words given to them from God, or they use prophecy to make their own opinions known. However, if you think of prophecy in terms of your relationship with God, you will speak only what you sense He is saying, and you will learn to interpret everything through your relationship with your loving and kind Father.

When you begin to practice using your prophetic skills, it feels like a guessing game at first. However, becoming secure in your own identity as a beloved son or daughter whether you get it right or wrong will enable you to keep practicing. It helps to start in a safe community with friends or family who give you lots of grace. After a while, you will get better at knowing whether or not you have something from God; you will sense a weightiness or maybe you will have just a "knowing." Whether you are certain or not, stepping out in faith and taking a risk is the only way you can grow.

Sometimes, when you are around prophetic people or at a prophetic conference, a prophetic anointing is flowing and you will be able to receive prophetic words more readily and clearly. I think of the future king Saul in the Old Testament. Probably he had never prophesied before, but he started prophesying when he was surrounded by prophets, to the point that people asked, "Is Saul also among the prophets?" (1 Samuel 10:11). Like attracts like and who you hang out with does make a difference. We are so blessed to live in a time when we have so many amazing prophetic men and women we can learn from firsthand or through books, the Internet, and classes.

Paul told the members of the church in Corinth: "Eagerly desire gifts of the Spirit, especially prophecy" (1 Corinthians 14:1, NIV). I believe that this gift is a priority because we need it in order to be equipped to love and speak to the hearts and spirits of both pre-believers and believers in powerful and anointed words.

Giving God's encouragement, strengthening, and comfort (what we call "practicing the prophetic," see 1 Corinthians 14:3) is essential for evangelism. God communicates with us in many ways but prophecy is a language of the heart, built on love.

Some have been called to the prophetic "office." Theirs is a leadership gift meant not only to be more widely than in the local church but also for equipping others. The office of prophet is a gift from God and He bestows it on whomever He chooses. However, all of us are invited to eagerly seek prophecy, and God would not have asked us to seek it if He didn't intend to make if available to everyone who wants it.

"Eagerly seek" implies that you might need to practice. Building your prophetic muscles is part of your relationship with a loving God because it is so important to be able to hear what He says. You may not be called to the office of prophet but you are certainly called to prophesy.

Prophetic Games

We have used several prophetic games to help us practice. The general rules for these games are as follows: (1) Give words that are encouraging, strengthening, or comforting—period. No warning words or words that predict dates or mates or specific guidance. (These can be valid, but they are not for beginners.) (2) Filter all words through love, with discernment. Otherwise, even positive-sounding prophetic words can be harmful.

I knew a very charismatic and good-looking couple who were dating, and everyone seemed intent on predicting that they would get married. Even strangers at prophetic churches would stop this couple to say they saw them married. However, this didn't work out and today both of them are happily married to other people. If you are moved by outward appearances and your own ideas of what looks good, such "drive-by" words can be harmful.

When you give spontaneous words to strangers, you must be guided by simple prophetic etiquette: Tune in to God's heart for this particular person, only stating what you sense in the moment and not adding to it, not letting your own opinions or prior experiences influence the word. And do everything in love. It is a good idea for even more experienced prophets to first run specific words of warning or direction past a leader.

If you perceive something negative, turn it into a positive word. Ask God for help. For example, as I mentioned in chapter 3, if you sense a pornography problem in someone's life, then call out the opposite: that he is meant to be a man of righteousness, holiness, and integrity toward women. He already knows his sins. God wants you to call out his destiny in Him. Let the Holy Spirit do the convicting and that will lead to repentance. It's God's kindness in letting us know we are loved and accepted that leads to repentance. After all, He died for us while we were yet sinners.

"Circle Up the Wagons" is a fun game for a group of people. Make an inner circle and an outer circle of people facing each other. Have the people in one circle close their eyes while the other circle walks around until you tell them to stop. The people with eyes closed give a prophetic word for the person across from them. They keep their eyes closed so they won't know who they are prophesying over and won't be distracted by what they may already know about this person. Next, have the other circle of people close their eyes and take a turn to give words in the same way. In a group setting like this, people who don't think they are prophetic can start encouraging the person across from them. Soon, it gets hotter and hotter in the Spirit and the loves flows even between strangers. It usually starts with some awkwardness and turns into hugs all around as people feel blessed and affirmed. It is my favorite prophetic game because people catch on so quickly—and because the Holy Spirit wants people to succeed.

"Random Photos": Find random pictures of trees, places, houses, rivers, or just about anything and spread them out on a table or floor. People choose a photo, look at it and ask God to give them a prophetic word, a Bible verse, or a thought to write on the back. You can give them to each other, or you can take them with you to give out on the streets. (You also can collect them and let the group pick just one to share.) It always amazes me how specific the words are for someone's situation. Our awesome God wants to communicate with each of us in powerful ways.

"Random Objects" is a game to get people thinking in symbolic language. Gather different household objects and put them in a bag. People pick out an object and then give a prophecy relating to this object. For instance, if I picked out a key I might say, "God has given you a key to open many doors and you already have it. It is the key of love. He will give you high favor to unlock hearts with love and the doors He opens no man can close." Short and simple. You are practicing listening to the Holy Spirit for a word and then delivering this word to someone in your group. This can be surprisingly effective in launching people into using God's symbolic language of the heart that can be so impactful.

"Pictures of Tattoos": Beauty and art are in the eyes of the beholder, but the Holy Spirit can give you specific insight about a tattoo that will touch someone's heart and connect them with Him. Usually, people get tattoos that have a particular meaning or symbolism. By interpreting their tattoos prophetically, you can open up their hearts to hear more. Ask God for revelation and wisdom as to what the tattoo means to the person and then ask Him for His interpretation. For practice, find a selection of photos of tattoos and encourage each other to step out of their comfort zones. Interpreting tattoos can be a good way to focus on interpreting things in a positive, strengthening, and loving manner that is specific for the person you are delivering the word over.

"Art, Dance, Music": You can practice drawing or painting, dancing, or singing under the prophetic guidance of the Holy Spirit. All you need are some art supplies or a source of music. Untrained artists, dancers, and musicians can be encouraged by others who have more experience as they learn how to open the eyes of their creative side to God's inspiration, moving to the heartbeat of heaven, making the supernatural natural.

"Popcorn Encouragement" is probably the most fun to do with a person whose love language is words of encouragement, but it works for anyone. Who isn't blessed by affirmation from God? Pick one person to stand in the center of the circle. Everyone is to give one encouraging word for that person. It usually starts slow and then heats up like popcorn popping. In our society, where people make an art of being sarcastic, we as believers need to counteract the stream of negative input by speaking the truth in love. I have seen many people in the middle start weeping as they are affirmed, loved, and encouraged. It goes beyond their minds and into their spirits. This exercise also gives a group unity as you hear the different giftings of each individual expressed in loving ways. People can start walking in their identity when they know it is appreciated and affirmed in love. We all operate better when we are celebrated, not just tolerated.

However, you want to practice, *just do it!* When you make a priority of listening to God and asking for a word, it becomes a lifestyle. When it is your lifestyle, you can reach out to others in love with a word of blessing for them anytime, anyplace.

*   *   *   *   *

On our way back from a mission trip to Ukraine, my son and I felt that God was saying we were not finished yet, and that we should make a stop in Jerusalem before we went home. So we went to Jerusalem.

As we were riding the train from our hotel in the suburbs to the Western Wall and Old City, I asked a young girl sitting beside us where we should get off, and she let us know with alarm that we had missed the right stop. She offered to show us the way and asked specifically where we were headed.

I told her that we were going to start at Church of Holy Sepulchre and proceed along the Way of the Cross. She had no idea what I was talking about, but said she had been thinking of going to that same church, too. As we walked, she explained that she didn't get out much but wanted to visit this church to curse an old boyfriend. This started an adventure with us asking God for words for this dear, brokenhearted girl. Apparently, she had been living with a guy who said he was a Christian. He had cheated on her and had left her. Since then, she had been very depressed, staying in bed and not leaving her apartment or bed for months. She had been seeing a counselor who asked her to come to his office for appointments just to get her out.

As we walked to the church together, we spoke words of hope and encouragement over her even though we didn't know her full story yet. Because of the insights from God that we shared with her on our walk, she stayed with us for the entire day and dinner that night. At the Church of the Holy Sepulchre where she had said she wanted to curse her former boyfriend, we asked her if she could forgive him instead.

At first she said she couldn't, but as we spoke words from God that softened her heart, she began to shake. She chose to forgive this man, who she said had stolen her youth and ruined her life. She was only thirty-one years old, but so depressed and suicidal that she thought her life was over. After she was able to pray out loud with us to forgive him, she fell to the church floor weeping. I sensed we were to do some deliverance right then and there so we did. She got delivered of a death wish and depression on the stone floor in a little alcove of this beautiful church, among all the tourists and tour guides.

Next we went out into the streets together and followed the Stations of the Cross. This Jewish girl had never heard of them before, in her own city of Jerusalem. She asked, "Why did they whip and beat Jesus? What did He do to deserve that? At the Pool of Bethesda, she got healed of body aches and pains. She marveled at her healing and wanted to know if Jesus did this for everyone. Finally, at the Western Wall she said the salvation prayer, asking Jesus to be her Messiah, Savior, and Lord of her life.

We took her out to dinner and found out she was anorexic and hadn't eaten a meal in public in years. She got deliverance and inner healing for that as we sat overlooking the beautiful Jerusalem skyline at a patio restaurant. What an honor and joy it was to carry God's heart of healing, deliverance and love to this woman. He sent us to Jerusalem for forty-eight hours so that one woman could be set free and come to know Jesus the Messiah.

This divine appointment left her and us changed forever. She now reports that she goes to King of Kings church in Jerusalem every Sunday and is growing in her faith. She says it was the love that attracted her to two strangers on a train. The prophetic words sealed the deal and the rest was God's plan of salvation for someone who had never read the Bible before but who lived the Way of the Cross that day.

Application Prayer

Dear Lord, let me always be ready to love the people around me in power, word, and deed. In this broken and hurting world, you are the light in the darkness. Increase my desire to hear you and to bring the light of your unconditional love to those around me. Surprise me with daily divine appointments that change my life as well as the lives of others. In Jesus' name. Amen.

Chapter 8

Word of Your Testimony

There is a difference between your testimony and history. You gain spiritual authority by the power of the word of your testimony. Share your story and see God's power come alive in your life.

*W*hat *is the best thing that has ever happened to you?* This is a very subjective question. It also is a great opening for sharing your personal testimony. After you carefully listen to someone answer this question, in turn you can ask if you can share the best thing that has ever happened to you.

The story of how you came to Jesus (your testimony) is unique to you and no one can argue with it. Your story is important to share. Many people think either that their testimony is not worth telling unless it is sensational or X-rated, that it is just too ordinary and boring to be of interest to anybody—or that it is too shamefully X-rated to tell at all.

It's about time that we know that each person has a story to tell, whether bad or good. God says in His Word that we are overcomers by the blood of the Lamb and the word of our testimony (see Revelation 12:11). There is authority and power in sharing how encountering Jesus has set you free to be uniquely *you* in spite of everything. The blood of the Lamb is an extraordinarily powerful force. When you call upon Jesus to use your testimony, you put it "under the blood" and it goes out in unbeatable power.

Storytelling

Storytelling has long been an important form of art and communication. Long before people could read or write, there was the spoken word. Stories were told and retold by generations to pass on knowledge, comfort, or encouragement.

People can usually remember a story far better than other words. When a story is anointed with the power to transform because of the blood of Jesus—look out! It goes on and on into eternity with power.

We are instructed throughout God's Word to tell our children about what God has done so that His faithfulness can be written on their hearts and minds. It is important to actively recall about God's faithfulness in bringing us this far. Too often we talk about what the enemy has done instead of telling about God's faithfulness. We need to remember and talk about how God reached down to us and set us free because of the blood of Jesus.

My younger brother died suddenly shortly after he turned forty. He had been a loving and kind little brother but as a young adult he became mentally ill with adult-onset schizophrenia. He was brilliant, creative, very musically talented, and had excelled in college. He had married the love of his life, then divorced her after a short time. Most of his adult life, he was in and out of mental institutions and on psychiatric medication. He was not himself, which made it difficult to communicate with him. We loved him; prayed and fasted for him; tried deliverance, counseling, and breaking off generational curses. When he died, I was asked to be the main speaker at his funeral and to give his story.

As I asked God how to share his tragic life story, I felt He was saying that I should focus on God's faithfulness. Our family was struggling with losing my brother twice—once to mental illness and then to death. As I looked for God's faithfulness in his life, I saw a pattern. My brother had been brought up by a family who loved him, in a home where Jesus was honored and we were a part of our local little church family and neighborhood. He had asked Jesus into his life as a ten-year-old boy, and had been baptized. Even though many years later mental illness would take his mind, God had never left him. God is always faithful to the end. I believe that we will see him healed and whole in heaven.

Focusing on God's faithfulness healed us as a family and it helped answer some questions. Some people had wondered if he would make it to heaven, because he was so crazy and withdrawn at the end of his life. The Holy Spirit reassured me that God's faithfulness had seen my brother through to the very end and into eternity, because of the blood of Jesus. His testimony will always be one of God's faithfulness in the midst of heartache and loss.

Timeless Testimonies

Future generations can hear your testimony and be set free. There is no stopping anointed words from flowing into eternity by whatever means He chooses. As you take the time, energy, and effort to form your life story into a powerful testimony, ask the Holy Spirit what He wants you to say or write. Listen and then let your unique personality show as people see Jesus through your transformation.

What if you still are struggling in certain areas of your life? You were meant to go from glory to glory, not five steps forward and then six steps backward. Of course it is all right to make mistakes, as He is so much bigger than all our mistakes, but what do you do when you feel stuck or aren't able to gain victory? Ask the Holy Spirit to point out any hindering spirits that keep you from breakthrough. Ask Him to put the focus on what He wants you to communicate. Ask Him to establish your true identity in Him and how He sees you. Remind yourself in God's Word what He says about you. You were made to be an overcomer, one who finds your core identity as a beloved son or daughter of the King. As you tell your story from this overcomer's point of view, you encourage others to also find breakthrough in their lives by trusting Jesus.

When I say "hindering spirits," I am referring to anything that needs to be broken through so that you can live in liberty. This may include generational curses, an orphan spirit, your own psychological state or mindset. As you walk through your own testimony, notice if you can see a pattern of something that holds you back. Unforgiveness, anger, bitterness, trauma, rejection, or taking offense can all hinder you from moving forward.

Your testimony should be glory to glory, or fresh to fresh. It is not so much a matter of getting saved at a certain age but it is the ongoing revelation of life with Jesus, empowered by the Holy Spirit, growing as a beloved son or daughter of your loving Heavenly Father.

Your History Is Worth Telling

Your history is the factual story of your life. It may include where you were born, your family, your life experiences, and even feelings you have experienced. Your history can have trigger points that bring pain and hurt to the surface. In other words, your history of trauma, wounds, and hurts—if they are not dealt with—can trigger painful memories. It is important to seek inner healing for the trigger points in your history. You are not a victim, but rather an overcomer.

Sometimes wounded people get lost in sharing their history with others because they have not yet been healed of an experience or have agreed with the lie of the enemy about being a victim. A victim spirit will usually leave you feeling powerless to change and preferring pity over compassion. Getting healed is a process and it's all right to acknowledge that you are still dealing with issues. The important part is that you are looking to Jesus, the author and finisher of your faith.

The living Jesus is the only one who can change your history into a testimony. The circumstances and facts will always remain part of your history or story but He will bring new hope, peace, and transformation. You are not your history, but you are your testimony after meeting Jesus.

In God's Word, you will find a treasury of life-changing words that He wants you to not only believe but also speak and decree and declare over yourself, as well as others. Get familiar with the Word of God, so you can turn to God's truth at all times. You are the head, not the tail, and you do not have to be jerked around by the enemy. We don't fight against flesh and blood, but spirits. No weapon forged against you will prosper and every lying tongue will cease. You have been crucified with Christ and He lives in you. You can do all things through Christ who strengthens you. The enemy is under your feet and you are seated in heavenly places. He knew you when you were still in your mother's womb and you have a destiny. He is singing a love song over you.

In writing and rehearsing your personal testimony, you may discover points where you feel shame, discouragement or confusion. Let these triggers be covered by the blood of Jesus through inner healing, counseling, or mentoring. God will never shame you. "There is therefore now no condemnation to those who are in Christ Jesus, who do not walk according to the flesh, but according to the Spirit" (Romans 8:1). He will bring conviction and you can confess, repent, and be set free of anything that holds you back from being all you are intended to be.

The enemy is always accusing. The Bible says he prowls around like a lion looking for some way to get in and torment you (see 1 Peter 5:8). The good news is that you can ask God if there is anything that you need to confess and repent of and when you do, the enemy will have no more legal right to torment you. Go up into the courtroom of heaven and ask our just and fair God for justice. When you know that God's mercy triumphs over judgment and Jesus has paid the price for every sin, then you can approach the throne by the blood of Jesus. Your loving Father always wants the best for you and He wants to give you good gifts.

The enemy of your soul is always lying and telling you that you don't measure up, are not good enough, or that no one wants to hear from you. Don't agree with those lies.

Decide now to ask the Holy Spirit to help you write your testimony with power. You are made to climb mountains with sure-footed confidence in Him alone. There is only one you, and you are unique and special.

One-Minute Testimony

As you share about how Jesus has changed your life and what He means to you, try to do it in one minute. People seem not to have very long attention spans or they are too busy to listen. Make it brief, but personal. Tell as briefly as possible about your life before Jesus, what happened to change your life, and then summarize your life with Jesus. (Of course, if you have been invited to speak at greater length, you can highlight more parts of your story.) Here is a start:

"My life seemed without hope and I didn't have inner peace. I was confused as to my identity and felt something was missing. Someone told me how Jesus changed their life and how He gave them a new love, hope, and peace. I wanted that, so I asked Jesus to come into my heart and be Lord of my life. I confessed and repented of going my own way. He really did start changing me from the inside out. You can do this as well. It's all about accepting Jesus and His love for you, by faith."

Your testimony can be very simple and it does not have to be exciting or X-rated. (However, if you do have an X-rated testimony, don't be ashamed to share it. Give God the glory for changing your life and giving you new life in Him.) Sometimes people raised in godly homes who have never rebelled but who have been seeking God most of their lives feel as though their testimony is not sensational enough to catch someone's interest. But God always uses the pure in heart. What a joy it is to be able to tell of God's faithfulness in your life. What a blessing to share about how obedience brings blessing and how, even though you were raised going to church, you had to make that decision for yourself and choose Jesus.

Every testimony is powerful when told from the heart and anointed by the Holy Spirit. And remember, no one can argue with your unique and personal story.

Usually, the more simply and concisely you can tell your testimony, the more effective you will be. You are not trying to talk anyone into believing, but rather to briefly share your faith journey. The Holy Spirit will anoint the words and He will do the rest. You are not selling Jesus or trying to make a sale or a deal. You are not trying to bring conviction; that is the Holy Spirit's job. He is more than capable of bringing conviction.

Often when you are talking, people will start weeping, saying, "I don't know why I am crying. I never cry but just can't help it now." Tell them that is the Holy Spirit touching their heart in a personal way. You are simply sharing a life-changing event and asking if they would like to encounter this life-changing and personal God through Jesus.

Approach people with a smile and ask, "What is the best thing that ever happened to you?" Listen. Ask if you can tell them the best thing that has ever happened to you. Share briefly in one minute: (1) What your life was like before Jesus, (2) What changed your life? (3) What your life is like after coming to know Jesus. Then, (4) tell them how to come to Jesus and/or lead them in praying with you to encounter Him.

You may be led by the Holy Spirit to elaborate on what He has done to set you free, transform and restore you. Focus on His love and His power. Give the praise for what He has done and let His great love for people shine through. You want to leave the person thinking about Jesus and how He changes lives, not your personal history.

However, that being said, He often will highlight something you say in your testimony that will catch someone's attention or that they can identify with. God will use your openness in sharing from your heart. No matter what you have been through, there are people who can identify with your words. The Holy Spirit who has ordained the connection will anoint your words. Go ahead and talk about your addictions, sexual abuse, tragic losses, infertility, miscarriages, divorces, or any other life hurt. He will use it as you are open and honest.

Giving your one-minute testimony can be a powerful way of planting the seeds of salvation in others.

*　*　*　*　*

We once went to visit some families to invite them to a function that we host in the Godtown neighborhood. One of the women on our team had recently been in jail and had just been released from a halfway house. She was eager to share her story and see others set free. As the man of the house came to the door, we chatted and invited his family to come join the cookout. He wasn't really interested, but said he would send his kids. I asked our team member if she would like to share her testimony with him. As she shared about the hurt and shame of being locked up, wanting to get out, trying to start over and staying free, he began to cry. He said that he had recently been in jail and that he wanted things to be different this time for his kids' sake. We were able to share that only through Jesus changing his life and giving him the power to overcome would he really succeed. The word of her testimony was very life-changing as well as very specific for that man.

*　*　*　*　*

I was in Belfast, Ireland with a group of young adults from Godtown. Four of us were to share our testimonies at a small church where most of the members were over sixty years of age. One team member told her story of dealing with rejection until she was set free by Jesus from this trigger. Another had been sexually abused by a family member and told what she described as an X-rated story. Another told of how God had saved his life after a car accident and how Jesus had given him hope. Male and female, different ages, different stories. But the common thread was how Jesus sets us free, transforms us, and empowers us to live a victorious life.

Those testimonies opened the door for so much more to happen. People received both physical and inner healings as they felt freer to open up to breakthrough and transformation. The testimonies invited the anointing of the Holy Spirit to come.

Words of Knowledge and Testimonies

No matter how brilliant you are, everyone has limited knowledge about many different subjects. Only God knows all things; He has perfect knowledge on all things. He is the source of what we call words of knowledge—those thoughts or ideas that God will impress on your mind or heart concerning things that you didn't or couldn't know by yourself. It is not the same as your opinion or something you already learned about. You just suddenly know something and wonder, *Where did that come from?*

The Holy Spirit wants to guide, comfort, and nurture us even as a father guides his beloved children. His thoughts may not be our thoughts, but we can accept them and be influenced by our awareness of what the Holy Spirit is impressing on us. This information is beyond us. It isn't like women's intuition or human discernment; it really is the Holy Spirit revealing information for us to use.

The word of knowledge is a gift of the Spirit that is available to all, and it is much needed. The more you acknowledge that you hear and the more you act accordingly in obedience, the more you will hear. I use the word "hear," but usually it is more of an inner "knowing." You just know that you know, but you are not sure how or why you know.

Too many of us miss these inner knowings or pass them off as just fleeting thoughts. We need to ask for words of knowledge and pay attention to the brief and momentary thoughts that cross our minds. Even if you have never been taught how to listen to the voice of the Spirit, it's not too late to start.

I believe that God wants to talk to His children on a regular basis, not just day to day but moment to moment—even in the middle of giving a testimony. It is vital to navigate by aligning ourselves with Him, listening to Him all the time. Learn to listen and catch the smallest nudge or inkling about things in your daily life, so that you can be ready to receive more and more. Words of knowledge can cover anything from trivial things like, *Where did I put my keys?* to life-changing words. You can ask God for a word of knowledge about anything, confident that He loves you and wants to speak to your heart.

Even doctors with many years of education and experience say that they are "practitioners" who practice their particular field of medicine. We too need to practice all the time. God desires to speak to His children and wants to communicate more than you want to hear Him. Remember, He often speaks with just a whisper or slight innuendo, so don't miss those fleeting thoughts from Him. He can and will use all kinds of ways to communicate with His beloved children.

Words of knowledge can even reveal specifics such as addresses and phone numbers of strangers. This can be useful in getting people's attention, because it certainly points out the fact that a loving God knows all about them.

* * * * *

Recently I was ministering in a prayer tent at a Christian music festival. A young lady came in on crutches asking for prayer for the healing of her ankle. She had been bitten by a spider and her ankle was red and very swollen as well as painful to walk on. We asked her what her pain level was on a scale of 1 to 10, and she said 10.

We prayed in Jesus' name that her pain would leave, the swelling go down, the itching leave, and healing come. As we prayed, I heard the Lord say, *Ask her about her relationship with her father.* When I did, she replied that her dad had died when she was ten years old. He had been a good daddy and she missed him.

The Holy Spirit then led me to ask her if she had been able to forgive her dad for abandoning her, explaining that although he had not intended to die and leave her, to a ten-year-old girl it sure felt like abandonment. As I led her in a prayer of forgiveness, the Holy Spirit highlighted certain points in time that her dad had missed: when she turned sixteen and started to drive, when she had graduated from high school, and more. Each event that was mentioned in the prayer brought more tears to the eyes of this precious young woman. As she wept, healing flowed both spiritually and physically.

When we looked down at her ankle, the swollen redness was subsiding and the pain had gone. She walked away with a new heart and healed ankle, set free by the Holy Spirit through simple words of knowledge.

*   *   *   *   *

Once I was in a restaurant with a friend and we both knew prophetically that we would be served by a waitress with tattoos. We had asked for words of knowledge concerning this waitress and were looking forward to interpreting her tattoos. (My friend and I love to interpret tattoos. We know that nobody puts permanent art on his or her body unless it means something personal.)

Sure enough our server had several tattoos—aliens, stars, moon and sun. She said she was getting more tattoos soon.

We noted that she seemed very interested in the supernatural. She agreed, mentioning that she was very interested in ghosts, too. We got into a conversation about supernatural things, God, and the occult. Like so many people, she had so many questions and nobody to ask. She could readily find information about the dark side of the supernatural world but not about God. Talking about supernatural things should be natural for believers.

She kept coming back to our table to talk. She listened as we very briefly shared a one-minute testimony. She was working and didn't have time to listen at length. (God can move in hearts in a nanosecond and we don't have to explain the entire Bible beforehand.) She loved it when we told her that God loved her "to the moon and back" because she was a single mama who understood a parent's love for a dear child. It was only a short time before she asked us if we would pray for her.

Step Out in Faith

Step out in faith, share a word of knowledge, and let the Holy Spirit move in people's hearts. If you do this in love, they usually respond with tears and heartfelt thanks. Engaging others with a word of knowledge is fast and cuts to the heart of things. When they encounter someone who will share Jesus with them, they will know the truth and the truth will set them free (see John 8:32).

Of course, as with anything prophetic, we must remember the "rules of etiquette." Even if you think you have gotten a word of knowledge that predicts marriage partners, wait for the Holy Spirit Himself to speak to the parties involved and you don't have to help Him out. Never tell someone who they are supposed to marry—especially if it is you. Because I work with young adults, I have often heard of both girls and guys telling someone: "God told me you are 'the one,'" or they describe a dream about marrying a particular person. In that kind of a situation, trust God to let the other person know, don't try to convince anyone about God's choice; this is your own manipulation and control at work.

I have also had people come and ask me to discern whom they are to marry or something specific for their future. It always seems best to steer them to seek godly counsel from trusted mentors, to draw close to God in intimacy, and to ask Him personally. We have been invited to ask for wisdom and revelation (see Ephesians 1:17 and James 1:5).

Prophecy should affirm what people already know in their hearts. It is not fortune-telling or the occult predictions of a psychic. It is not for us to be the ones who are in the know and so that we can exercise power over others. If someone keeps asking you to seek God for them, that will keep that person from becoming close to Him and also can cause overdependence on you. It may also give you a false sense of importance to be the one who "knows" things. God loves a humble heart.

Words of knowledge and words of your personal testimony open the hearts. They are meant not only for pre-believers but also to encourage believers. Testimonies build faith, encourage others, and set you free to share your heart without holding back. Determine now that you are going to ask the Holy Spirit to sharpen your storytelling skills so that your testimony can be a powerful tool to be used to share with anyone at any time.

Application Prayer

Dear Lord, you love me, you know who I am, and you enable me to testify of your faithfulness to me. Thank you that you want to set me free to use my words to influence others for your Kingdom. Set my words on fire with your love. Through my words, may people taste and see your transforming power and goodness. In Jesus' mighty name, amen.

Chapter 9

Hunger for the Supernatural

People are hungry for supernatural experiences. Jesus said those who believe will do greater things than He did. Let's give them a double dose of Jesus—His amazing character and glorious power.

Getting to know the Holy Spirit personally is one of the most amazing adventures you will ever have in your life. The Holy Spirit is not an "it," but the third person of the Trinity who always points to and glorifies Jesus. Supernatural things will become natural as you get to know the person and power of the Holy Spirit.

When I refer to "the supernatural," I mean anything that cannot be explained by the laws of nature. Our society often portrays the evil side of the supernatural. However, God is above all things. He is over everything natural and everything we call supernatural. He created the laws of nature and all of the things humans can see and figure out. But He Himself is not limited to natural laws. He can do whatever He desires. The supernatural is natural to God, and walking in the supernatural is a natural part of growing in the Holy Spirit.

Hungry for More

Your hunger for the supernatural attracts all of heaven. Jesus told us to hunger and thirst after righteousness (see Matthew 5:6). The Bible makes it clear that the righteous will live by faith not by sight (see 2 Corinthians 5:7). Your faith will motivate you to search out the One who is the Author and Finisher of your faith (see Hebrews 12:2). He has prepared a table for you in the presence of your enemies (hindering spirits) so that you can follow God alone (see Psalm 23:5).

The spiritual hunger that comes from God produces a desire for more of His supernatural presence. This is nothing like a striving or an insatiable appetite for the approval of your fellow believers but rather a deep desire to be all that God has created you to be, a willingness to go where He goes and to do whatever He tells you to do. This includes moving in every gift of His Spirit, breaking through the spiritual darkness with His light. We are meant to taste and see that the Lord is good and introduce others to their destiny in the Lord as His beloved children.

* * * * *

Once we were in a restaurant and asked our waitress if she would like prayer. She said she wasn't religious so she didn't believe in prayer, but she did have a migraine that was making it difficult to concentrate on her work. She was a single mom and needed her paycheck. She couldn't afford to go home sick, so she was trying to get by. But she was losing focus because of the pain. We prayed for her; all the headache pain left. We gave her a few prophetic words about her destiny, and she asked if we were psychics. We told her that the healing and the personal words came from the God who loved her and who had sent us to get her attention. These signs made her wonder about God, and she asked Jesus to come into her heart as Lord of her life. We kept in touch with her. She got filled with the Holy Spirit and is doing well in growing in her faith.

Presence-Filled Atmosphere

Like Moses, you can say, "Unless you go with me Lord, I am not moving" (see Exodus 33:15). But don't just sit; it's hard to steer a rock. Listen. Ask the Holy Spirit to bring you guidance, boldness, and motivation. Then, as He leads, move forward.

Yes, unfortunately sometimes we go off under our own steam. Nothing happens. It is important to not run ahead or behind, but right in sync with the Spirit. We need to learn to listen to Him and then move accordingly.

We were made to take God's presence with us in powerful ways everywhere we go. I especially love to go out on the streets of the inner city doing ministry with the presence of God. It's always an adventure.

One time, we went to a local high school to prayer-walk the halls. We had met with the principal earlier to ask how we might be of help to her. In prayer, I had seen that particular school with the words "strategy" in neon lights over the school, so I was expecting an all-at-once download from the Spirit of the heavenly strategy for this outreach. Instead, the strategy was revealed over time. First we were given permission to prayer-walk the building after school hours. In the halls, we met a teacher who invited us to meet in her classroom after school, where we could invite students to come for encouragement. Step by step, a group called The Refuge emerged. We took the name from a verse in the psalms: "God is our refuge and strength, a very present help in trouble. Therefore we will not fear" (Psalm 46:1–2).

Each week, we met and prayed and listened—and obeyed as He brought the right people into place. We needed a teacher as a sponsor and yet for the club to be student-led. The students who came once a week and began to participate were very shy people. However, over time, they stepped up to lead, which was way outside their comfort zones.

God's presence is still leading and we are still following. The strategy is still evolving but we are thankful for what is happening to change this inner-city high school and the staff and students.

One of the students went with us on a summer mission trip to London and Belfast this past summer. He had never been on a plane and certainly not outside the country. He had to raise his own funding to go on this mission trip, just like all the participants. His family doubted that he could raise the money, as it seemed monumental. However, he wrote on Facebook for all to see: "If Jesus wants me to go then I will get the money."

The teachers at his school saw how he had changed over the school year into an emerging leader and they all got behind him to raise the money. Some gave him items that he didn't have such as a suitcase. The mission trip consisted of street ministry in the Hindu/Muslim neighborhoods in London as well as neighborhoods in Belfast, Ireland. The teachers wanted to hear all about his trip, as they were invested in it.

God always has a comprehensive strategy; all we have to do is listen and be obedient to His plan. He says through the prophet Isaiah, "if you are willing and obedient, you shall eat the good of the land" (Isaiah 1:19).

When I first went out on the streets trying to do ministry, I was timid and it was very hard for me to see myself being used to heal someone or set them free or give a word of prophecy. I did have compassion for the hurting and wanted to be used to set people free physically, mentally and spiritually, and I know that this desire came from God.

I was part of a telephone counseling ministry with a couple of friends who started going out on the streets every week in a very diverse neighborhood. I went along with them. In just a few short blocks, we counted eighteen countries that were represented. There was a Muslim mosque, several Muslim grocery stores, and a Tibetan monastery (one of only a few in the States). Residents representing several South American countries were there, all trying to make it in America. Each week we would see people healed and set free, miracle after miracle. We knew that God had brought these dear people to our country so they might be introduced to Him.

Most of these immigrants were hardworking and intent on making a living for their families. God would highlight the ones we were to talk to and we would approach them in love to pray for their needs. God's presence was strongly with us as many people got healed, set free, and got jobs after we prayed. His presence was so powerful that often people would just weep or strangers would walk up as we were praying, wanting to hold our hands.

We grew in our ability to move in the supernatural by making ourselves available to be used by the Holy Spirit. We noticed and got rid of any hindering spirits that were holding us back such as fear of failure or fear of what people think of us.

Greater Things

We remembered Jesus' important statement—that His followers would do greater things than He did:

> Most assuredly, I say to you, he who believes in Me,
> the works that I do he will do also; and greater works
> than these he will do, because I go to My Father. And
> whatever you ask in My name, that I will do, that the
> Father may be glorified in the Son. If you ask
> anything in My name, I will do it. (John 14:12–14)

What does He mean by "greater works?" That statement is meant to remain wide open and to make us hunger and thirst for more of the supernatural. The Holy Spirit leads us to step out boldly in faith. With God's Word as our measuring device for what is true, we see the words "greater things" in His Word and our faith springs into action. We move and breathe in our relationship of faith with the One who spoke those words.

On my own, we are not able to heal anyone. However, we can depend on what God's Word says: "By His stripes we are healed" (Isaiah 53:5). When we ask for a supernatural anointing of the Spirit and step into the supernatural realm, we find that "with God all things are possible" (Matthew 19:26).

*   *   *   *   *

God always does more than we expect Him to. I was with a group of people on a mission trip to my beloved Ukraine, where I have dear friends. We were doing ministry and I was teamed with a young man who had been away from doing any ministry for a while. A Ukrainian man came up to us and asked for healing prayer for his back, which he had injured in a bad motorcycle accident. He also told us that he was worried and anxious about his wife's pregnancy, as their last baby had died at birth. He confided after some prayer that he had cheated on his wife and felt that the baby's death was punishment for his sin. He loved his wife and really wanted to be a good daddy. As we prayed over him, I laid my hand on his lower back and my hand became very hot. It felt like it was on fire. He felt it also, exclaiming about the intense heat. My partner said that he could see a big blue hand of an angel over my hand.

The Ukrainian man got totally healed from all back pain and delivered from all anxiety. He said that he felt like a new creation. He asked Jesus into his heart to help him be the husband and father that he was created to be.

My prayer partner was ecstatic and he continued to pray over people, seeing many healed. This was a multiplication of blessings: a young man who had walked away from his faith was revived; a young husband's heart was changed, his badly damaged back healed physically; many others were healed and changed, repenting of their sins and set free to follow their loving Father God. Only a God who loves people and wants to see them set free displays so many supernatural miracles at once.

Amazing stories like this increase our faith. "Faith comes by hearing" (Romans 10:17) and then you can step out in faith and pursue with the Holy Spirit all that God has in store for you. God does not withhold one good thing from those who ask in faith, reaching out to Him for more.

Relationship, Not Religion

It's all about being in a relationship with Him. Out of this relationship will flow a love for people that will motivate you to desire to move in the supernatural. Look for a good ministry training school in your area. Find online videos or books that help you understand how you fit into the big picture.

Ask the Holy Spirit to lead you in your growth. God's Word says that we can ask for wisdom and He will give it abundantly (see James 1:5). Ask for knowledge, revelation, and breakthrough.

Confess and repent of not believing that God wants you to move in supernatural signs and wonders—wonderful evidence of a powerful and personal God for both pre-believers and believers. He wants you to be transformed more and more into His image as you move "from glory to glory" (2 Corinthians 3:18), ever exciting, fresh to fresh, deeper and deeper into a supernatural relationship of love and obedience to the living God.

Jesus paid dearly on the Cross so that more supernatural wonders could be manifested in the world through those who believe in Him. He told His followers that they (we) would do greater supernatural things, because He was sending His Holy Spirit to empower us to move in His gifts. When we step out to move in signs, wonders, and miracles, we have all of heaven cheering us on!

Application Prayer

Lord Jesus, you shed your blood on the cross to allow us to come into your supernatural realm. The most supernatural experience of all is seeing someone receive eternal life through salvation. Show me how to move naturally with supernatural grace to move mountains by faith, to see the captives and prisoners set free, and to heal brokenhearted people. Signs, wonders and miracles all are possible because of you, Lord Jesus. Show me what this looks like! In Jesus' mighty name, amen.

Chapter 10

Taste and See—Using Your Senses

God has given us senses with which to discern His goodness. We can learn to use all of our senses in discerning how to give away His love.

In the student union on the local university campus, Tuesdays are set aside for different clubs to advertise for new members. Two young men with their faces buried in their laptops sat behind a sign that read "Atheist Club . . . Best Damned Club on Campus." I thought this was hilarious, and one Tuesday I approached them. Week after week, I would come back and chat with them, always asking if they needed prayer for anything. Of course, they would point at their sign and we would all laugh.

However, God began to give me words for their hurting and broken hearts. They had to do with never knowing a father's love and wanting love, affirmation and acceptance and that the father of one of them was a pastor and their relationship was strained, at best. I delivered each word with compassion for them, as I really liked them personally, I appreciated their sense of humor, and could feel their hurting hearts. As the weeks went on, each Tuesday they would began to close their laptops and wait for me to give them a prophetic word.

This was all well and good, but Christmas break was coming and they would be graduating. I knew that I would probably never see them again after they graduated. I was all right with letting them go but something compelled me to pursue them more. The Lord told me to ask them what their favorite cookies were. I was to bake them peanut butter and chocolate chip cookies so that they would "taste and see" that the Lord is good. Armed with compassion and the cookies, I asked if it would be OK to give them a word about their destiny. One looked up, interested, so I told him what I had heard from God. His dad was a pastor and he had watched as a church split left his family wounded and hurting. His dad had been unfairly accused and criticized by controlling and manipulative people. As a result, this young man wanted nothing to do with organized religion or God.

He asked how I knew this, because it was right on. I told him that God wanted him to know that His own Son was wounded and hurt by religion and that God isn't a fan of religion, either.

The words I gave his friend touched his heart, also, and he teared up when he heard them. He had lost family members in an accident that left him alone and hurting. He was mad at God and wanted no part of organized religion. Prophecy softened their hearts but they still weren't ready to open up to all God had for them.

I handed each one a box of the cookies I had baked them, explaining that God had told me to make them so they could taste and see that He is good and that it is His kindness that leads to repentance. Now, you have to remember that these were two college guys who were away from home. Their hard hearts had started melting from prophetic words but I guess their love language was food (gifts) as they both came around the table to hug me. Then the tears started flowing as a mother's love broke through their pent-up hurt and anger.

Sometimes, the Lord uses the smallest things to let people taste and see His great love for them. Compassion compels you to go the extra mile in loving people into the Kingdom family.

Aroma of Christ

Second Corinthians 2:14 reads, "Now thanks be to God who always leads us in triumph in Christ, and through us diffuses the fragrance of His knowledge in every place."

Taste is just one of our five senses. What are the others? Smell is another way that God gets our attention. Sometimes smells and fragrances are good and sometimes they are bad, and the Holy Spirit shows us their significance if we are paying attention.

Did you know that evil spirits have smells? I found this out once when I was in a prayer room with a group of people in an old, rodent-infested building. I had brought my beloved dog with me. Mocha was sniffing around when we all closed our eyes to pray. All of a sudden, someone blurted out, "I smell the death spirit." I opened my eyes to see poor Mocha eating rat poison that someone had put in a corner under the table. I was able to rush my dear pet to the nearby vet so that he could give him charcoal to eat. He threw up the poison before it did any harm. Because someone had discerned— with their sense of smell—the presence of evil, my dog's life was saved.

People often will smell sage or other smells when witchcraft is present. It is like Holy Spirit radar to detect the enemy and a good reminder that "He who is in you is greater than he who is in the world" (1 John 4:4). When you smell something suspicious, pray and claim the blood of Jesus over whatever it may be. Practice using your sense of smell and ask the Holy Spirit how to use it.

Seeing Is Believing

Our sight can be either our biggest disadvantage or our biggest advantage. We can see what is real in this world but having eyes for the spiritual world takes faith. We are not to walk by sight, but by faith.

Practice looking and asking God to show you people through His eyes. Look with His eyes of love into those you meet. You are meant to call out the gold in those around you. Remind each person of who God says they are meant to be. Encourage them.

Don't go by outward appearances, which can be misleading. Keep the eyes of your heart open to what God is doing in the Spirit and you will be able to see it. He is a Light on our path and He guides the way.

The Word says, "Lean not on your own understanding; in all your ways acknowledge Him, and He shall direct your paths" (Proverbs 3:5–6). The Hebrew word for "acknowledge" is *yada,* which is an intimate kind of knowing. In other words, stay intimately connected to Jesus and He will give you eyes to see. It's all about the relationship with Him.

"I pray that your hearts will be flooded with light so that you can understand the confident hope he has given to those he called—his holy people who are his rich and glorious inheritance. I also pray that you will understand the incredible greatness of God's power for us who believe him" (Ephesians 1:18–19, NLT).

Touch

There is something about a hug that encourages people and makes them feel accepted. I once asked God about hugs and He said, "Hugs brush off the dust of the world." As I meditated on this, I realized that, as humans, we have been made to be affirmed through appropriate touch. A pat on the back, an arm around a shoulder, holding hands, hugs—all are encouraging when led by Holy Spirit.

However, the enemy has hijacked the sense of touch to make it seem negative, leaving many afraid to use touch appropriately. Studies show that babies deprived of touch will be diagnosed with a condition called "failure to thrive." We need to affirm each other but also be mindful of those who have been harmed by inappropriate touch.

I know girls who don't like to be in crowds because of past hurts involving touch. When we have been wounded, it is easy to put up walls and harden our hearts protectively. Yet touch is considered to be one of the five "love languages" and can be a major tool for breakthrough when Spirit-led.

The Spirit touches our hearts with music and beauty and other senses. Why not be open to His touch? Let God protect your heart, as He is a good Daddy and wants to protect you, provide for you, and call out your identity.

Sometimes you might feel the weight of God's presence. Ask Him for revelation during these times. Sometimes, He wants you simply to soak in His presence and feel loved. Other times, He will give you an assignment and you will know you didn't just think it up. Being aware of His touch can help you move accordingly, with your eyes a little more open to the spiritual world around you.

Hearing

Jesus said, "But when He, the Spirit of truth, comes, He will guide you into all truth; for He will not speak on His own initiative, but whatever He hears, He will speak; and He will disclose to you what is to come" (John 16:13, NASB).

Just as the Holy Spirit listens and obeys what He hears, so should we, as believers who are filled with the Spirit. We can hear from God in our hearts because He has made it possible. Jesus also says, "My sheep hear my voice" (John 10:27). He speaks to us in dreams and visions or writes on your imagination. Sometimes, your "knower" just knows what He is communicating. Only very rarely do people hear an audible voice.

Whenever you pray, spend time listening; don't do all the talking. Your prayer should be a two-way conversation. Your good Papa always wants to communicate with His beloved children.

As you learn to listen to God's voice, practice obeying as well. When you aren't sure what to do, ask Him and He will reveal to you His intent. To find His direction in important matters, fast and pray. Fasting sharpens your spiritual sense of hearing. How long should you fast? Until you get the breakthrough you need, or the assurance of it.

Starting Out

When our children were young, I had a great desire to hear God more clearly. During their naptime, I would pray and listen for God to speak to me. I read the only book I could find at that time about hearing God (along with the Bible) and it encouraged me to listen. I was in a church that didn't believe in God speaking and this book was written by a pastor in this particular denomination. *Hearing God*, by Southern Baptist Pastor Peter Lord, changed my life.

As I was learning to listen, I thought I heard the Lord say, "I want you to make a cherry cheesecake and take it to the new woman you met on Sunday." Well, I had one of those Jello cherry cheesecake mixes in my cupboard so making one would be easy, but I didn't know the woman's name or where she lived.

I called our Sunday school teacher and she told me that we'd had three new people that day. Which one was she? We decided which one it might be and I got her address. When my daughter woke up from her nap, I put her and the cheesecake in the car and off we went in search of this address.

Now, this was thirty-eight years ago, before GPS or online mapping, and I had trouble finding her house. When I did find the address, I started thinking, "I'm not even sure I heard correctly. I don't know if she is even the right person and I don't know what to say."

When I asked God what I was supposed to say, I only got a sense that I was *not* to say "Welcome to our Sunday School," or something like that. I wanted to be obedient, so I went to the door.

I rang the doorbell, hoping that no one was home. I heard someone coming to the door. As she opened the door, I could see that she was indeed the right woman I had sat beside on Sunday, and I also saw that she had been crying. I blurted out, "God told me to give this to you," and handed her the cherry cheesecake. She looked startled and confused and promptly slammed the door in my face. I heard crying on the other side of the door, so I slunk back to my car.

Somehow I had upset her and I should be embarrassed. I wasn't sure what had just happened so I drove away and put it behind me. Shortly afterward, we moved away and I didn't think about it anymore.

However, three years later we moved back to the same little town. A friend in a Bible study asked me if several years before I had taken a cake or something over to this person. She asked me why I did that. Now, I was hoping no one knew of this and here she was questioning me about it.

So, I explained how I had been trying to hear God and felt that He had told me to go give her the cheesecake. I explained how she had slammed the door in my face and I had somehow upset her and how I never did understand it.

My friend explained that her husband worked with this woman. They were the ones who had invited her to church that day when she sat beside me. At the time, this woman was going through a rough period in her life and struggling in her marriage. She usually wouldn't have been home in the day, but she had taken the day off work. She had been sitting in her living room and had just prayed, "God if you are real, then please show me." *Bing-bong*—there I was at her front door saying "God told me to give this to you." She was completely undone. Now she knew that God was real and that He knew her intimately. She even loved those Jello cherry cheesecakes. Now, three years later, she was being discipled and growing in the Lord.

Soul Senses and Spirit Senses

Each of us consists of body, mind/soul, and spirit. God said He created us in His image and we are wonderfully made. Instead of running after popular trends, I need to exercise my spirit to rise up and be in charge over my body, mind, and soul, looking to Him to understand what He has ordained since the beginning of time.

God is raising up people who will not fit in with the world's ideas of what looks good or right. He has a plan and a purpose for every life. Don't be misled by what you see or sense in your mind, body, and soul but stay focused on what the Spirit is saying to your spirit. Those are the only things that matter and they are the things that will last.

Some people have special needs because of physical or mental disabilities. However, their spirits are not disabled. When you speak to their spirit directly, the Holy Spirit can call them out of darkness into God's light.

We need to learn how to see, taste, smell, feel, and know in the Spirit, and we need to trust in the Lord with all our hearts to bring it to pass.

People are held captive by false beliefs about others, themselves, and God. Only the truth will set them free. You were made to carry the love and truth of Jesus to others so that they can be transformed into the people they were meant to be.

Purpose and Assignment

Your God-given destiny and purpose has been established in heaven. Books and personality tests can help you discover your purpose as you pray and seek God's will for your life. Seasons of life change and ministry assignments come and go, but your purpose remains the same.

My purpose may be to encourage people to fulfill their true destiny through knowing God and being transformed. My assignment may be teaching and equipping people, telling people about how much God loves them so that they can come to know Him. My purpose comes from Him, and so does yours, although our specific assignments may change over time as we grow and develop.

When you move in an appointed time in obedience to what God is calling you to do, you have power. You may not even know why you are doing it. You may not feel equipped or ready.

You may not want to be doing it. However, when the King of kings asks you to step into an adventure with Him and you say "yes" in obedience, you will succeed. All the world may laugh at you or tell you that you don't fit in, but when you are obedient to Him and your desire is to please Him, you are exactly where you should be.

You can't give away what you don't have, so you must be filled to overflowing in the Holy Spirit. Knowing your destiny and purpose will help you move forward in bringing God's Kingdom to your sphere of influence, but the only way to successfully choose between the good and the best is to listen to the Spirit. Sometimes you may not be sure but just stepping out in faith will put you into His presence so that you can proceed accordingly.

Gospel of the Kingdom

John the Baptist proclaimed repeatedly, "The Kingdom of God is at hand." Jesus preached of the Kingdom of God as he healed the sick, cast out demons, and set captives free. What is this Kingdom? The wonderful gospel of salvation is part of it. However, it also includes heavenly signs, wonders, and miracles. Because Jesus has already paid for our sins, we can live a supernatural life here and now. We cannot add to His finished work on the cross but we need to appropriate its power in our lives.

The Gospel message gets people saved and going to heaven. However, as we live here on earth, our God-ordained purpose is to bring transformation to people and to restore them to the relationship of their Kingdom family. Restoration and transformation are part of the plan for every person because of God's great love.

Not everyone will be saved but God wants them to be. The Word says that He "wants all people to be saved and to come to a knowledge of the truth" (1 Timothy 2:4, NIV). The enemy has been defeated, but he is still accusing and looking for ways to hinder us and block us from coming to God.

When people come into the presence of God, they often feel hope and peace. The world is desperate for this. When we bring God's hope, love, joy, and peace to a hurting world outside the church doors, it awakens people's desire to know the Living God.

We bring God's presence in simple but powerful ways when we stop for someone who is hurting with even one kind, encouraging word. Such things leave behind a hunger for more of Him because they change hearts.

God has sent each one of us to refresh, restore, and renew the world around us. It is up to us to ascertain what He wants us to do today.

Application Prayer

Dear Lord, here I am, ready to go wherever you send me today. Thank you for placing me just where you want me at just the right time. Help me to bring a taste of heaven to somebody who needs it. Through me, bring your Kingdom to the people I meet. Shine your light into the darkness through me. In Jesus' strong name, amen.

SECTION 3

Go and Do Likewise

Chapter 11

You Have a Green Light

Jesus did only what He saw the Father doing. You were created to do likewise, moving in His love. What are you waiting for?

You have been given a green light to step out in love. So get over yourself, step out in faith, and *go*.

Don't take time to focus on yourself; it will only waste time and energy. Instead, focus on Jesus and ask Him what is holding you back. Don't let mistakes hold you back—they are an important part of your practicing.

As you practice, don't be discouraged if you see results only now and then. It will become more consistent as you trust Him. You were made to move in full confidence in Him.

As you pursue healing, prophecy, and miracles, both your passion and your compassion will increase. You will begin to see breakthroughs, because they are part of your destiny, created as you were by your heavenly Papa to move in love as a world-changer. Jesus died so that you could be free to join the world-changers in the service of His Kingdom. By pursuing a closer and deeper relationship with the risen Jesus, his compassion and power will become yours and will produce signs, wonders, and miracles.

You have been given the word "go" and you can ask for the spiritual gifts that you need. The gifts are for everyone: "Follow the way of love and eagerly desire gifts of the Spirit" (1 Corinthians 14:1, NIV). God's Spirit wouldn't have inspired Paul to write "eagerly desire" if He didn't mean it.

You might not be called to the office of prophet, but you and every believer are called to love the person in front of you. And if that person needs a miracle, then you are *it*. You don't have to take them to some special meeting. Just be yourself and move in whatever He has called you to do. Step out in faith that you are the one called today to bring the Kingdom to the person in front of you. When you sincerely love people and want to encourage them, He will make a way for this to happen through you.

If you were walking by a lake and heard a drowning person calling for help, what would you do? Using the nearest boat or life preserver, you would act quickly to save that person. You wouldn't say, "Hey, I know a good lifeguard at my church. Come with me next Sunday and he will help you." No, in an emergency situation you do the best you can yourself. If you feel that something is hindering you, get the inner healing, counseling, mentoring, or prayer ministry that you need.

Curses

Curses hinder you from fulfilling your God-given destiny. Sometimes you can be your own worst enemy by repeating and agreeing with the lies of the enemy. (When you agree with the enemy's lies, you become the second witness against yourself. It takes only two to convict.) Ask God to help you identify the lies from the accuser so you can stop agreeing with them and ask Him to show you the opposing truth so you can start agreeing with Him instead. In His Word, find out who He says you really are and start telling yourself those words. Declare and agree with prophetic words spoken over you.

You might be suffering from generational curses that you don't know anything about because you weren't even born when they began.

God can reveal in a dream if you are harboring something that keeps you "triggered." You may dream about a past wound and realize that you have been bound by fear ever since. By watching someone else or reading something, you may recognize an unhealthy pattern in yourself. The Holy Spirit will reveal what you need to know about yourself—and what you can do about it, especially if you ask Him. You don't need to strive to figure it all out.

Where you have sinned, confess, repent, and agree with God that you have done something wrong. Tell Him you are sorry and ask for forgiveness. Once you have sincerely repented, these curses will not be able to stick to you anymore: "Like a fluttering sparrow or a darting swallow, an undeserved curse does not come to rest" (Proverbs 26:2, NIV).

The enemy is legalistic and if he can find another way to steal your joy and destroy your destiny, then he will. Steer clear of his lies!

Getting Free

I come from a long line of godly men and women who lived with integrity—pastors, prayer intercessors, denominational Sunday school superintendents, God-fearing folks who loved the Word of God. However, also in the family line are early and untimely deaths, miscarriages, and mental illness. I can't know all the dark secrets of my ancestors, but I can break off, in the mighty name of Jesus, any curses associated with Freemasonry, hatred, unforgiveness, occult practices, broken covenants, lies, or whatever he shows me, even back to Adam and Eve.

Once when I was reading a book about overcoming generational curses, I started having very specific dreams for several nights in a row. Every night, someone (I'm not sure who) would bring up a sin of mine or my family and I would just agree with what he said, confess the sin, and repent of it. It seemed like I was doing battle in the Spirit for my family. I knew it was an answer to my prayers and woke up each morning feeling refreshed and empowered.

However, on the fifth night, I dreamt that I was in my parents' old bedroom in our old house. I knew that the number "five" represents grace and that bedrooms in dreams can represent intimacy. The room had yellow walls as my parents' had and it looked just like their room. To me that indicated "family and ancestors."

In this dream bedroom, there were thousands of moths on all the walls, floor and ceiling—about three feet thick. I had never seen so many moths in all my life. Somehow I knew in the dream that each of these moths represented a family sin or curse that the enemy had a legal right to hold against us. I was overwhelmed. The previous nights it had simply been a matter of agreeing as He brought each specific thing up, and it was overcome by the blood of Jesus.

This time it just seemed endless and I couldn't see how I would ever get free of all this. In the dream, I cried out to Him for help. Suddenly, someone handed me a tiny little bottle that held only one drop of something red-colored. I heard, "pour it out." I thought to myself, *I need a whole lot more than just one little drop*, but decided to be obedient.

It was one drop of the blood of Jesus and, when I shook it out of the bottle, it created a whirlwind that ridded the room of all the moths, cleansing every issue out of my heritage. One drop of the blood of Jesus can cleanse us of all our sins, even the generational ones. The Lord says,

> Though your sins are like scarlet, they shall be as
> white as snow; though they are red like crimson, they
> shall be as wool. If you are willing and obedient, you
> shall eat the good of the land. (Isaiah 1:18–19)

I continued to obediently confess and repent of all He showed me. All I ever needed to do was to claim the blood of Jesus. I did not need to strive for perfection. I did not have to figure out hidden secrets that were too deep to be discovered. All I had to do was to rely on Him. Over time, He washed my family line as white as snow.

Your personal history will always be whatever it is. However, when you are set free from the automatically triggered reactions to the rejections and sins of the past, your history becomes like a harmless file stored on your hard drive. It is important part of who you are, but it no longer sparks fear of rejection or shame or a host of other issues.

God can use you just as you are today. However, getting free is transformational. Equipped to move in authority and power, you are sure of your identity as a beloved son or daughter of God, and it no longer matters what others say. You can move forward, knowing you are celebrated, not just tolerated. In a very real way, you are transformed into a superhero in the supernatural power of His love, and you can bring breakthrough wherever it's needed in everyday life.

*   *   *   *   *

I have taken many people out on the streets to witness, only to have them tell me they were just going to watch, not participate. One young man came with us because he was attracted to a young lady on our team. Gabe said that he wasn't really interested in witnessing or prophecy but he just wanted to hang out with us and watch. I countered that if he was there at all, then God had called him by name and had sent someone for him to talk to. He wasn't so sure of this.

We went by a school building and a teen was sitting on the steps. We thought he might be a student and stopped to talk with him. He was sixteen years old and had just come to the United States from Norway for a two-week visit with his American father, who was divorced from his mom. He spoke good English. He had a guitar with him and he was trying to strum a new song he had heard.

Gabe said he knew that song and he could show the Norwegian teen how to play it. They struck up a conversation. Gabe asked his new friend where in Norway he was from. The teen said it was just a tiny little town that no one ever heard of. However, when he told us the name of the town, Gabe got very excited. It turns out that the town is where all of Gabe's relatives came from, and he had visited there just the previous summer. This opened everything up.

Gabe prayed with the teen and they exchanged names and email addresses. The boy might have come for only two weeks to see his dad, but God had another Father for him to meet. We told him that God had brought him all the way across the ocean to meet Jesus and to find a new relationship with his heavenly Father. Overcome with joy and laughing, this Norwegian teen was introduced to Jesus and the Holy Spirit.

As we walked back to a coffee shop, Gabe looked at me in awe and wonder. How did God know that he didn't want to witness, yet He had made it so easy? Gabe only had to show up and God showed up too.

Fresh Expectations

These kinds of amazing divine appointments are meant to be normal for us. Ask God to give you divine appointments every day and then be on the lookout for the people He will send to you. Life with Him is an exciting adventure.

You don't have to give up your "day job" to go into full time "Christian" work. You are a missionary wherever you are. Your lifestyle is one of hearing and obeying. As you step into the supernatural way of doing things, you will begin to see people differently, not ever as targets or trophies to be won, but rather as beloved sons and daughters that Jesus is longing to bless through you with His compassion.

As you move through your days, you will see people highlighted in the Spirit and you will just have a "knowing" that you are supposed to engage them. Although you might not know what you are going to say, you will find that as you start to converse, things will open up. You might get a word of knowledge, a word of wisdom or prophetic word. You might feel that you are supposed to offer to pray for physical or inner healing. You might need to do some deliverance along the way. Or you might just need to listen to their story and give them a hug.

Whatever it is, as you are obedient and keep practicing, you will be able to say, like the seventy-two disciples when they returned, "even the demons obey us." A world of folks out there need what you have to offer. If you don't feel equipped, then start getting equipped now with the tools I have been describing in this book. Don't hesitate or delay: "Indeed, the 'right time' is now. Today is the day of salvation" (2 Corinthians 6:2, NLT).

God uses us even in our weaknesses. In fact, He says our weaknesses qualify us. Jesus says, "My grace is sufficient for you, for My strength is made perfect in weakness" (2 Corinthians 12:9). So we can respond, as Paul did: "Therefore most gladly I will rather boast in my infirmities, that the power of Christ may rest upon me. . . . For when I am weak, then I am strong" (2 Corinthians 12:9–10).

I think this qualifies us all.

Green Light Go

If you feel that you have to wait to be more equipped then you will be waiting a long time. But as you step out in obedience, you will see that you can trust God to do what He will do and you are just a willing piece of the puzzle.

When Jesus said the harvest is ripe so pray for workers (see Luke 10:2), He was talking about you and me. We can trust Him to use us to His glory. We only have to be willing. Before long, it becomes a natural thing to move in His love and to splash over on everyone around you.

Many times, you will be anointed to get recompense for the very types of things that have hurt or affected you personally. If you have suffered addictions, a religious spirit, miscarriages, broken covenants—whatever has come your way—you can both win victory over it and then share the victory with someone else. When someone hears that you also have been down the same road and now have victory because of Jesus (even if you are still in the process of getting free), you are powerful. Each of us is a work in progress and we are growing and learning from Him every day.

Always remember that hunger that attracts the Holy Spirit. If you are hungry for more of His life, you will be fed. Refuse to allow discouragement to take root in your heart but instead push into your own breakthroughs with Him. He will show you what you need to know. He wants you to fulfill your God-given purpose and destiny more than you do!

Application Prayer

Dear Lord, thank you that not only have you authorized us to go, but you have equipped us with the power of your Holy Spirit and surefooted confidence in you alone. Fulfill your will today in my sphere of influence. Thank you for putting me in the right place at the right time. As it is in heaven, let it be here on earth where I live. May your Kingdom come. In Jesus' mighty name, amen.

Chapter 12

Agree, Align, Advance

God spoke the world into being. The merger of our speech and physical action brings supernatural power to bear on the world around us. It's time to move out in love, power, and authority.

It's time to agree with God that all things are possible with Him. Jesus said, "With God all things are possible" (Matthew 19:26). All things means all things, in every language and in all circumstances.

So many people put up with pain because they don't know God can heal or deliver them. Many don't think He even cares. This is true for both believers and pre-believers. "That's just the way it is," they say, which is the same as agreeing with the lies of the enemy.

When we encounter difficult situations or health issues that look hopeless, we have the joy and privilege of speaking life over death, healing over disease, and hope over hopelessness.

* * * *

Once we were waiting for a bus at the end of the day when a lady slowly limped by us on the sidewalk. She looked so tired, carrying her bags and grimacing in pain. We stopped her and asked if she needed prayer for anything (not wanting to point out her limping at first). She questioned what we meant and who we were and then wanted to know where we went to church. All these are normal questions, as we were strangers to her and she didn't know why we had stopped her.

I explained that God had highlighted her to us and that we felt He wanted to bless her. I inquired about her limp and she said that she had gotten so used to her hip hurting that it was part of her. I asked her, "Do you want to be healed?" She didn't answer, and we continued to chat. The Lord said to my spirit, "Ask her again if she wants to be healed," reminding me that there is a power in agreement. I asked. She stopped and hesitated and then said, "Yes, I guess so."

As we prayed in Jesus' name, "Be healed," her pain left, and she felt renewed both physically and spiritually. Her entire demeanor changed, and she was so happy. She said that she lived alone and no one ever seemed to notice her. She just existed day to day, hoping to make it through each day without more problems.

What a difference one encounter with Jesus makes. She now had renewed hope that things could change because she was a beloved daughter of God. Her faith was renewed and she said that she would never be the same.

Agreeing with God

Over and over in His Word, God tells us that He is for us, not against us and that His love endures forever and ever. He will never leave us or forsake us. He says that if we move toward Him, He is always there.

Agreeing with God is really just saying OK when He whispers in your heart, "I love you." When the Holy Spirit brings conviction to our hearts and we simply agree, confessing and repenting of anything that hinders our liberty in Him, we overcome the power of sin and the evil one.

When you agree with God, you can know that He will finish what He has started in you. You can trust Him as you to move forward in faith to do anything and everything He asks of you.

There is much power in words of agreement. Agreeing with God changes things.

It doesn't matter what personality type you are or how you react to the world. What matters is that you agree with God as to who He says you are as a beloved son or daughter who can do all things through Christ who strengthens you. No one is telling you to change your unique, God-given personality. However, if you agree with God, He may take you outside of our personality to empower you to do all that is required for His glory to be displayed on earth.

In Genesis, Eve agreed with the serpent and her sin brought death into the world. In the New Testament, Mary agreed with the angel of God, saying, "Let it be to me according to your word," (Luke 1:38) and she was used to bring Jesus into the world.

In the Old Testament, it always took two witnesses to convict a person. When we agree with the enemy, we become the second witness against ourselves or our family. The enemy will always accuse—and will always look for your agreement. That's why we should never speak negatively about another person. When we do that, the enemy can bring it up before God's throne saying, "Even her mother/father/friend says he is never going to change." What comes out of our mouths is powerful.

The enemy is always looking for a legal right to accuse. We can confess and repent of any negative thoughts or words spoken and break off our part of that agreement. The enemy comes only to kill, steal and destroy (see John 10:10). Why should we help him by agreeing with him?

Let's agree with God, the One who is always speaking life and love over you and your family. Speak life over yourself, your family and others.

As believers, we want to be in agreement with the rhythm of heaven. We want to adopt a Kingdom mentality. The Word says, "If you are willing and obedient, you shall eat the good of the land" (Isaiah 1:19). That sounds good to me!

*   *   *   *   *

A certain young lady in our ministry would rather be doing contemplative prayer alone and in silence than being called upon to engage with strangers on the streets.

One time we were sitting in a storefront church in London, watching crowds of people go by on the street. Suddenly she got hit with the idea that God wanted her to head out onto the street corner. Intentionally, she agreed with God's assessment of her as a person of worth who should share the Good News in public.

Without hesitation, she went up to people and asked if they needed any prayer for healing or a miracle. She had so much joy, her face was glowing.

Soon, a young man came by and he stopped to chat with her. I went out to offer him some water and pray with them. He told us that he was recently homeless and was an immigrant from Croatia. He was lonely, scared, and thirsty. He didn't have proper documentation papers yet, although he had applied for them. This would take time and he was waiting to get the proper papers so he could get a job.

As we prayed and prophesied encouraging personal words over him, his heart was softened toward God. He came into the storefront church and was introduced to others who shared their stories of redemption. His heart had been wounded by the trauma of leaving his country and we prayed healing over his heart. Soon he asked Jesus to be Lord of His life and come into his heart.

He joined us for his first communion as a new believer, laughing and singing with joy in worship. Filled with the Holy Spirit, he could feel the presence of God. What a change from the depressed and scared young man we had just met on the street! Someone gave him directions to a shelter and we gave him some money. We prayed that he would get a job and be blessed financially.

He left with new richness of spirit, body, and soul. All this because one shy person decided to agree with God.

Agreement with God Brings Blessing and Unity

When we agree with God, we see people as He does. We are able to call out the gold in people instead of being critical or judgmental. The Word says that He is singing over us, and it is a love song:

> The Lord your God in your midst, the Mighty One,
> will save; He will rejoice over you with gladness, He
> will quiet you with His love, He will rejoice over you
> with singing. (Zephaniah 3:17)

Do you hear the love song sung over the world by Him? Agree with this love song and celebrate the gifts of God in others. Listen and ask Him what He is singing over you. It is always encouraging.

Ask God what He wants you to agree with Him about today. We sometimes ask God what grieves His heart so we can agree with Him. Shouldn't we also ask Him what makes Him laugh? With all of heaven, we want to celebrate the goodness of God, no matter what we are feeling about our personal circumstances. God is good all the time. There is great power in agreeing with Him.

Agreeing with Prophetic Words

Do you take seriously the words that have been spoken over you? Prophetic words are meant to hold an anointed weight that will produce fruit when we agree with them. If a reliable person tells you that you are going to be a great tennis player and you love to play tennis, then go practice. Sow into your prophetic word in agreement.

When you get a prophetic word, don't just hope and pray that it will come true. Don't be uncertain because of your own limited view of God or your own insecurities. There is so much power in verbal agreement. Receive those prophetic words. Try this: Stand in front of a mirror and speak the words out loud over yourself with your own voice.

One time, I was in a South American country where I had been asked to speak at a women's conference. I really wanted to see signs, wonders, and miracles as well as feel His presence but I was feeling very inadequate. I was alone in my room praying for power and confidence in Him alone—and that I wouldn't mess it up. I heard God say very plainly, "Get your prophetic papers out and read them aloud over yourself." Over the years, I had written out on yellow legal paper many inspiring prophetic words that had been given to me. I had them tucked away in the pocket of my Bible cover. As I read them out loud, I began to remember who God said I was and I decreed and declared those statements over myself. I remembered that He has called me by name and will never leave me. I remembered all the amazing things that He has done in the past. I also remembered that He is the same yesterday, today, and tomorrow, so I could agree that His power was not going to be limited by my weaknesses.

It worked. The conference was filled with many powerful miracles and much joy.

The Bible says that as a man or woman thinks, so they are (see Proverbs 23:7). So it's a good idea to change your thinking to agree with His thinking about you. Then speak it out loud—confess it. The ability to speak merges your spiritual and physical being. When you let your spirit be led by the One who loves you, your spirit in turn leads your body, mind, and soul to speak in love.

People throughout history have written and sung love songs to each other, and we sing worship aloud to the King of kings. It changes the atmosphere—and our own hearts—when we use our physical voices to agree with the truth.

The spirit world operates by a spoken economy. God spoke and the world came into being (see Genesis 1). We declare and decree a thing and it will be done (see Job 22:28). This is not a "name it and claim it" thing, but a heart thing. We tune in to His great love and then we speak out with His words empowered by the Holy Spirit. We praise Him. We do not curse ourselves or others. We seek to have our tongues under control of the Holy Spirit.

Agree, Align, and Advance

One time the Lord told me that if I was agreeing with Him I would need to move to where the blessings were flowing. I didn't understand until He showed me a simple picture of a double sink. The water was flowing from the faucet into one side of the sink but the container that needed to be filled was sitting empty in the other sink.

Now I know God can bless you anywhere and in any circumstances. However, it seemed that I was going to need to move, and this was hard for me. It was hard because I couldn't see the logic of leaving where I was ministering at that time, where I had friends and felt I was well situated. I knew that I had a choice to make and that those blessings might disappear if I wasn't in alignment with His will. I'm so glad I decided to move in order to be aligned with Him, because it brought blessings beyond my wildest dreams.

It's all about relationship. If we listen to His direction and trust Him for the outcome even when things make no sense to us, we will find His blessing. It is like being one in unity, bonded together. Then His blessings can flow. Being in a seemingly safe place doesn't prove anything. We need to be aligned with His will and positioned exactly where He has called us to be.

Advancement in the Spirit

Agreeing and aligning with Him brings advancement in the Spirit and liberation from all bondages to fear or anything else that would hold you back. Fear paralyzes us from moving forward. You were made to step out of the boat and walk on water—or to walk through the parted seas. You have to believe that you can trust Him. Step out with sure-footed confidence even when you can't see your feet and the wind is blowing. You are His and He wants to use you to help bring His heavenly Kingdom to earth.

In the book of Deuteronomy, God gives a pop quiz and then He gives the answer. "I have set before you life and death, blessing and cursing; therefore choose life" (Deuteronomy 30:19). What does this mean for you and me?

Choosing life may seem to look different in different situations, but for each and every one of us it means this:

Choosing life means having the God of the universe speaking into your life, daily.

Choosing life means having Jesus as your Savior and Lord as well as Holy Spirit giving you love, joy, peace, patience, kindness, goodness, faithfulness, gentleness, and self-control (see Galatians 5:22–23).

Choosing life means you live as child of God who knows that He is a God who provides for you, protects you, and calls out your identity in powerful ways all the days of your life.

You have been set free to be the best *you* on this earth. You were celebrated by all of heaven on the day you were born—no matter the circumstances surrounding your birth. Choose to believe it here and now: Your life counts, your identity is beautiful, and your purpose and destiny are significant.

Application Prayer

Dear Lord, empower me now to move forward in your love. Let me be so filled to full and overflowing with your love that I splash all over everyone I encounter in a naturally supernatural way. I declare with all of heaven that because of you, Jesus, I am a world-changer and history-maker. I was made to be loved by you and give that love away. In Jesus' name, amen.

About the Author

Vivian Strong Klebs is an author, Bible teacher, and evangelist. Her passion is to see people set free to move in every good gift that God has given them. She loves to see people start hearing God, moving in prophecy, dreams and healing as a means to share God's great transforming love. She believes this should be a lifestyle not just an event. Vivian and her husband of forty-three years have four children, three sons-in-love, and two amazing granddaughters.